COOKING WITH SHEREEN
FROM SCRATCH

Because You Can!

COOKING WITH SHEREEN FROM SCRATCH

Because You Can!

SHEREEN PAVLIDES

Creator of
the popular TikTok
"Cooking with Shereen"

PAGE STREET
PUBLISHING CO.

First published in 2021 by
Page Street Publishing Co.
27 Congress Street, Suite 105
Salem, MA 01970
www.pagestreetpublishing.com

Distributed by Macmillan, sales in Canada by The Canadian Manda Group.

25   24   23   22   21   1   2   3   4   5

ISBN-13: 978-1-64567-304-0
ISBN-10: 1-64567-304-9

Library of Congress Control Number: 2020948908

Cover and book design by Kylie Alexander for Page Street Publishing Co.
Photography by Ken Goodman

Printed and bound in China

To my husband, Andreas, you make me laugh, everyday; my son, Costas and daughter, Isabella, you inspire me to reach higher to teach you all things are possible through hard work.

TABLE of CONTENTS

Introduction

I first started cooking when I was thirteen. I was obsessed with creating through food. I began teaching myself early on by reading food magazines, watching Julia Child and the Food Network, working in restaurants and then finally going to culinary school in New York City, where I graduated with high honors. The creative process gave me life. Fast forward to later in my career, while I was working as an on-air guest on QVC representing cooking appliances. Cooking with Shereen came to life via YouTube, TikTok, Instagram and Facebook, after ongoing viewer requests for the recipes I demonstrated so I could share my "how to" cooking videos and passion for cooking from scratch.

Cooking from scratch is empowering, builds your confidence and makes you feel happy! I want to help you cook like a chef and feel like a rockstar in your own kitchen. Throwing a frozen meal in the oven doesn't bring joy. So we won't! You're better than that. Make it from scratch . . . because you can! You may be thinking, "I just don't have the time," and I get it; I'm a busy mom of two, run a household and manage a full-time career. But if I can do it, you can do it.

This book is for people who want to eat real food and feel good preparing it, using less store-bought junk! I'll give you my chefie tips along the way to create shortcuts without compromising quality. I'll introduce you to your new friend the freezer, which makes preparing homemade foods a cinch, so you're stocked and ready to cook. I'll show you how to cook ahead when entertaining for friends or for the holidays—there's no reason to cook à la minute. By cooking ahead and keeping everything warm in the oven, you'll be stress free and able to enjoy your own party. I promise it'll still taste delicious and you'll be totally relaxed, and that energy makes for great food. I never want you to feel stressed or overwhelmed, *evah!*

We'll make food from scratch from around the world by cooking everyday staples like homemade chicken stock (page 51) and pita (page 23). Yes, you can make pita with your own two hands! There's no comparison and it's much easier than you think. Now, if you're making a recipe but didn't prepare the stock ahead, donta you worry, you can substitute with store-bought, for now. I know when you finally get around to making the stock from scratch, it'll blow your mind. And with your friend the freezer, your cooking will be taken to a whole new level.

Throughout my career, I have developed and tested recipes for Fortune 500 companies and national food magazine test kitchens. I also interned and worked on the line at the Fountain Restaurant at the Four Seasons hotel, hustling alongside Philly's finest chefs that were complete food snobs. I say that proudly! I've bottled up those experiences to bring you the best of both worlds. Homemade food from scratch, easy enough for everyday cooking at home. When you turn into a food snob, wear the badge of honor proudly! Because you're fancy!

Grab your aprons; let's cook!

Hugs,

Chefie Tip:
I use Diamond Crystal kosher salt for all of my recipes. If you're using a different brand, please adjust the measurements to taste.

STARTERS *and* SNICKY SNACKS

Soup, salad or appetizers—which my husband, Andreas, calls snicky snacks—are a great way to begin a meal, but honestly, you could make these your whole meal if you wanted. I don't believe in rules when it comes to food or cooking.

The freezer is your friend, whether you make my Homemade Chicken Stock Two Ways (page 51) or an entire soup to freeze ahead of time. The dishes in this chapter are also easy to make and thaw quickly for a starter or weeknight meal. Pair them with a French baguette or my Housemade Pita (page 23) for dipping; it's super easy to make and tastes insanely good! And yes, I freeze the pita, too.

My Shanghai Chicken Salad with Sesame Ginger Vinaigrette (page 43) is definitely hearty enough to make a meal, if you load up your plate. You can also pair or top my Homemade Caesar Salad with Garlic Croutons (page 41) or Balela Salad (page 47) with grilled chicken, shrimp or fish during the week. Don't feel like you need to crank out a three-course meal every time you cook.

When cooking, go simple and fresh. It'll be delicious and it reduces stress when the prep is easy. A happy cook is everything! You can always add my Gruyère and Thyme Popovers (page 48) or a crusty Italian bread to make a meal a little more filling.

Snicky snacks are also great to nibble on when you're hanging out at the pool or if friends pop over for a cocktail (check out the Crafty Cocktails chapter starting on page 167). Whatever you choose to do with the recipes in this chapter, they'll be perfect!

FRESHLY ROASTED SALSA *with* FRIED CORN TORTILLA CHIPS

When I was creating this recipe, I first started with fresh, ripe Roma tomatoes. It was delicious, clean and fresh but it was missing a depth of flavor, so I decided to roast the tomatoes instead. WOW! That was it! I made this with some spice for *flavah*, but you can adjust it to your liking. Wanna increase the heat? Add the seeds from the Serrano chile and add one to two more chipotles in adobo.

Makes 2½ cups (660 g) salsa, chips serve 18 to 20

6 cups (1.4 L) peanut or canola oil

30 corn tortillas (5½-inch [14-cm] diameter), quartered

Kosher salt

2 lbs (908 g) Roma tomatoes (8–12 tomatoes), quartered lengthwise and pulp and seeds removed

2 tbsp (30 ml) olive oil

Fresh finely ground black pepper

1 cup (160 g) chopped sweet onion or white onion

To make the chips, add the oil to a 6-quart (5.7-L) heavy-bottomed pot and heat to 350°F (175°C), using a candy thermometer to check the oil temperature.

Working in six to ten batches, fry the tortilla wedges until lightly golden, 1 to 2 minutes per batch, while maintaining the temperature. Flip if needed halfway through the cooking time for even browning. Using a wok strainer or tongs, remove the chips to a paper towel–lined sheet pan. Immediately season with salt. Repeat with the remaining chips. You can fry them up to several hours ahead.

To make the salsa, preheat the oven to 425°F (220°C). Line a baking sheet with parchment paper.

Place the tomatoes on the parchment-lined baking sheet. Drizzle the olive oil over them and toss to coat. Season with salt and pepper. Roast them until slightly caramelized, 30 to 35 minutes. Let them cool for about 20 minutes.

While the tomatoes are roasting, place the onion in a medium bowl. Fill with cold water and set aside to remove the raw, harsh *flavah*, so you don't have onion breath. You're welcome (wink).

(Continued)

FRESHLY ROASTED SALSA *with* FRIED CORN TORTILLA CHIPS (*continued*)

1 small clove garlic

¼ cup (60 ml) freshly squeezed lime juice

1 Serrano chile, seeded (as desired) and roughly chopped

1 chipotle in adobo + 2 tsp (10 ml) adobo sauce

¼ cup (4 g) chopped cilantro

In a food processor fitted with the steel blade attachment, grate the garlic. Then add the lime juice and stir. The lime juice mellows the *gálick*. Drain the onion and add it to the food processor along with the Serrano chile, chipotle in adobo, adobo sauce and the tomatoes and their juices from the parchment paper. Season with salt and pepper. Pulse until the mixture is chunky yet slightly smooth, scraping down the sides periodically. Season to taste, then fold in the cilantro. Serve with the tortilla chips.

The chips will keep in a large zip-top bag for a couple of days. The salsa will keep in your refrigerator for several days in a tightly sealed container.

Chefie Tip:
This salsa is equally delicious on fish, grilled chicken or pork chops, too.

SPANAKOPITA TRIANGLES *with* PHYLLO PASTRY FROM SCRATCH

These are more like hand pies than small appetizers. Eat them as is or serve with a Greek salad on the side for the perfect lunch. Try your hand at making the phyllo from scratch; don't be afraid! It's a little involved but not hard, plus it makes this recipe friggen' mind blowing! If using store-bought phyllo dough, double up the sheets, using 1 (16-ounce (454-g)) package.

Makes 20 Triangles

2 (11-oz (312-g)) packages fresh baby spinach

1 tsp kosher salt + more for sprinkling

3 tbsp (45 ml) olive oil

1 extra large onion, finely diced

1 bunch green onions, sliced, light greens and dark greens separated

¼ tsp fresh finely ground black pepper + more as needed

Preheat the oven to 375°F (190°C).

Divide the spinach between two extra large bowls. As you add the spinach, lightly sprinkle it with salt after each layer you add. This will help to begin wilting the spinach while you prep the remaining ingredients.

Place an 8-quart (7.6-L) pot over medium heat. Add the oil. When the oil is heated, add the onion and the light green onion slices. Season with 1 teaspoon of salt and the pepper and sauté until tender, 5 to 8 minutes.

Add the spinach to the pot, pushing it down to fit. The pot will be loaded at this point, but donta you worry! Cover the pot and reduce the heat to medium-low to steam the spinach for 2 to 3 minutes. Remove the lid and begin tossing and rotating the spinach from the bottom to the top. Increase the heat to medium. Keep tossing and stirring until the spinach is fully wilted; once it starts, it happens quickly, 1 to 2 minutes. Remove the pot from the heat.

Line a bowl with two layers of cheesecloth. Place the spinach into the cheesecloth-lined bowl, and let set to cool. Once cooled, wring out all the excess moisture using the cheesecloth.

(Continued)

SPANAKOPITA TRIANGLES *with* PHYLLO PASTRY FROM SCRATCH *(continued)*

3 large eggs, room temperature

11 oz (312 g) good-quality Greek feta in brine, drained and crumbled

½ cup (30 g) chopped Italian parsley

½ cup (26 g) chopped dill

20 (9 x 14–inch [23 x 36–cm]) homemade phyllo pastry sheets (page 18) or store-bought (see recipe intro)

1½ cups (360 ml) melted unsalted butter, kept warm

Grab a large bowl and whisk the eggs. Add the dark green onion slices, feta, parsley, dill and the cooled spinach and season lightly with salt and a few cracks from the pepper mill. Stir until well combined.

Working with one phyllo sheet at a time, lightly brush the sheet with melted butter, then fold the sheet in half (vertically) creating an approximately 4.5 x 14–inch (11 x 36–cm) sheet. Dab the phyllo with butter all over and carefully brush to evenly coat with a thin layer, being careful not to rip the phyllo. As you're working with the phyllo, keep the remaining sheets covered with a clean kitchen towel, so the pastry doesn't dry out and crack.

Add a level ¼ cup (50 g) of the spinach mixture to the top-right corner of the long sheet. Don't overfill it! Fold the phyllo over the spinach mixture, slightly pressing down. Fold over to the left, slightly pressing down to fill out the triangle, then fold toward you, then fold to the right, creating a triangle, folding like a flag. Lightly dab with melted butter when folding, as needed.

Place the triangles on a rimmed baking sheet and brush the top and sides with butter. Repeat, making ten. Bake until golden brown and crisp, 23 to 25 minutes.

While the first batch is baking, repeat with the remaining ingredients and place the ten additional triangles on a second baking sheet. Follow the baking directions for the second batch.

Chefie Tip:
Buy Greek feta in brine, then crumble it yourself; it's creamier!

PHYLLO PASTRY *from* SCRATCH

Making phyllo from scratch is a bit involved but not hard, so set your favorite playlist, get the family out of the kitchen and enjoy this time for yourself! With patience, it's pure therapy and so rewarding! Your family will love it! A helpful tip: Lightly dusting the sheets with cornstarch between the layers as you work in batches will help them not to stick.

Makes 20 (9 x 14-inch [23 x 36-cm]) pastry sheets

3 cups (375 g) all-purpose flour

1 tsp kosher salt

1 tsp baking powder

1 tbsp (15 ml) olive oil + more for brushing

2 tsp (10 ml) white vinegar

¾ cup + 3 tbsp (225 ml) warm water, divided

⅔ cup (83 g) cornstarch + more for dusting

Line two rimmed baking sheets with parchment paper. Set aside.

Add the flour, salt and baking powder to the bowl of a stand mixer. Using a handheld whisk, mix the ingredients. Pour in the olive oil and vinegar, fit the mixer with the dough hook attachment and begin mixing on low speed. Slowly pour in ¾ cup (180 ml) of warm water while carefully pushing down the flour, using a rubber spatula until the ingredients begin to stick together, about 1 minute. Increase the speed to medium and mix until moistened, adding 1 to 3 tablespoons (15 to 45 ml) of the remaining warm water, a tablespoon (15 ml) at a time, as needed, until the flour mixture is no longer crumbly and begins to form a ball, 1 to 2 minutes. As soon as the dough forms a ball, stop!

Remove the ball from the mixing bowl and brush it lightly with olive oil to thinly coat. Weigh the dough ball and divide it evenly into 20 pieces, approximately 1 ounce (28 g) each. Roll each into small dough balls and place on one of the parchment-lined baking sheets, then cover with one dry kitchen towel, topped with one faintly damp kitchen towel, as you work.

Fold the overlapping towels under the sheet pan to securely cover, so the air doesn't create a skin on the dough. Allow the dough balls to rest for 1 hour at room temperature.

Add the cornstarch to a medium bowl, and using a sifter, lightly dust additional cornstarch (see Chefie Tip) over your work surface and a ½ x 24-inch (1.3 x 61-cm) wooden dowel (if you have one—you'll have better control using this versus a rolling pin).

Working with one at a time, dip and coat a dough ball in the cornstarch on both sides. Transfer it to your work surface and roll it out to approximately 5½ x 8 inches (14 x 20 cm), flipping it over about three times. Lightly dust it with cornstarch and place the first pastry sheet onto the second parchment-lined baking sheet, keeping it covered with a towel as you work. Repeat with another dough ball, then place the new sheet directly on top of the first pastry sheet, dusting lightly with cornstarch between the sheets. Each sheet should be approximately the same size. Keep them covered as you roll out the remaining eight. Repeat this process until you have ten sheets in the stack. The dough will slightly bounce back as you roll; this is why we will roll the dough out in baby steps and give it a chance to rest in between.

Lightly dust the work surface with more cornstarch, then place the ten sheets on the surface and lightly roll out the entire stack to stretch the dough, starting from the center, flipping over about three times, rolling out the whole stack to about 8 x 11 inches (20 x 28 cm). If you have added too much cornstarch, fleck the excess away with a pastry brush. Again, these are baby steps, before we completely roll out the pastry to the desired size.

Peel back, one sheet at a time, and lightly dust each sheet with cornstarch, then stack them back on top of each other; this will help prevent the entire stack from sticking together in one clump at the end. For the sheets in the middle, dust a little extra cornstarch to prevent sticking. Now we are ready for the final roll-out.

Roll out the stack of ten pastry sheets to a 9 x 14–inch (23 x 36–cm) rectangle, flipping the entire stack over two to three times. The pastry should be slightly see-through at this point. Peel back the first sheet and place onto a piece of parchment paper. Layer each sheet with the same size (or slightly smaller) piece of parchment paper, to ensure they don't stick to each other. Finish with another piece of parchment paper on top of the stack and loosely roll up the parchment-wrapped pastry crosswise. Loosely but firmly cover and double wrap the entire roll with plastic wrap and refrigerate.

Repeat all the steps with the remaining pastry balls. Let rest, 1 hour to 2 days, or freeze for up to 2 months. Thaw overnight in the refrigerator before using.

Chefie Tip:
When dusting with the sifter, dust from up high for light, even coverage.

BABA GANOUSH *with* HOUSEMADE PITA

I've found this Middle Eastern eggplant dip is best when made with a good-quality extra-virgin olive oil, so don't skimp, it makes a difference. Cooking the eggplant over an open flame gives this a freakin' amazing smokey flavor. But don't despair, you could also toss the whole foil-wrapped eggplant onto the grill or slice it in half lengthwise, brush the flesh with oil, place flesh side down on foil and broil until tender, 15 to 20 minutes, as an alternative.

Oh, and if you're wondering what a male eggplant is, he has a round dimple at the base. He produces fewer seeds, making him less bitter than the female, which has an elongated slit at the base.

Makes 2 to 2¹/₂ cups (500 to 620 g)

2 male globe eggplants (about 2½ lbs [1.1 kg])

Zest of 1 lemon and ¼ cup (60 ml) freshly squeezed lemon juice (from 1-2 lemons), divided

1 clove garlic

1 tsp kosher salt + more to taste

½ tsp fresh finely ground black pepper

¼ cup (60 ml) good-quality extra-virgin olive oil, divided

¼ cup (64 g) tahini

½ tsp cayenne + more for garnish

2 tbsp (2 g) chopped cilantro

Fully wrap each eggplant in foil. Place each directly on top of two separate gas burners and keep the heat between medium and medium-high. Roast the eggplants until tender, 15 to 20 minutes, turning each eggplant about a third of the way around every 5 to 7 minutes. Place the eggplants in a large bowl, leaving them in the foil to steam and release the excess moisture. Let cool about 20 minutes.

Add the lemon juice to a food processor fitted with the steel blade attachment. Finely grate the garlic into the lemon juice and stir. It mellows the *gálick*.

Remove the eggplant from the foil, discarding the excess moisture in the bowl. Scoop out the flesh of each eggplant (discarding the skin) and add it to the food processor. Add the salt, pepper, 2 tablespoons (30 ml) of the extra-virgin olive oil, tahini and cayenne and pulse, four to six times, just to chop and reduce the stringy texture, until the mixture is smooth with some chunks remaining. Fold in the lemon zest and cilantro and adjust the seasoning to taste.

(Continued)

BABA GANOUSH *with* HOUSEMADE PITA
(continued)

1 tbsp (6 g) chopped mint

Grilled or toasted Housemade Pita (page 23)

Sliced cucumbers and red bell peppers, for dipping

Scoop the mixture into a wide, shallow serving bowl and, using the back of a spoon, create a circular swirl through the baba ganoush. Sprinkle with a dash of cayenne for color and drizzle the remaining 2 tablespoons (30 ml) of the extra-virgin olive oil to collect in the swirl. Garnish with the mint, because you're fancy!

You can make this up to a few hours ahead and keep covered at room temperature. To serve, cut the grilled or toasted pita into wedges and/or serve with sliced cucumbers and red bell peppers on the side, for dipping.

HOUSEMADE PITA

I know what you're thinking: "GURL! You want me to make homemade pita?!" Yes! Because it's BETTER and you CAN! Your first attempt may be a learning experience, but by the second or third you'll move into pro mode, if you don't master it on the first try. The best part: Wait until you taste it. I'll keep my mouth shut and let you be the judge.

Use these to make chicken gyros or falafels. Or warm, grill or fry cut pita wedges and dip them in tzatziki (page 58), baba ganoush (page 20), balela (page 47) or hummus. You can even slice these in half and fill them with chicken salad, lettuce and tomatoes for simple, homemade sandwiches. Please note, not every pita will have a pocket, only the ones that fully puff when cooking—it is what it is.

Makes 8 pitas

3 cups (375 g) all-purpose flour + more for dusting

1 tbsp (15 g) sugar

2 tsp (12 g) kosher salt

1 (0.25-oz (7-g)) packet active dry yeast

1 cup (240 ml) warm water

2 tbsp (30 ml) good-quality olive oil + more for oiling

Safflower oil

Add the flour, *shugá*, salt and yeast to the bowl of a stand mixer and whisk, using a handheld whisk (it's easier). Fit the stand mixer with the dough hook attachment and turn on to medium-low (speed #2) while pouring in the warm water and the olive oil.

Push down the flour mixture as needed until all the ingredients come together and begin forming the dough. The dough will be very sticky at this point. Continue mixing until the dough pulls away from the bowl and becomes smooth—this will happen quickly. Remove to a lightly floured surface and knead the dough until it is no longer sticky and when pinched with two fingers feels tacky but doesn't stick to your fingers, 5 to 6 minutes, lightly dusting with flour as needed.

Grab a large bowl that leaves enough room for the dough to proof. Lightly brush olive oil inside the bowl. Add the dough to the bowl and rub a little olive oil over the dough to evenly coat with a thin layer. Cover the bowl with plastic wrap and place in a warm place to proof until it doubles in size, 1 to 1½ hours.

(Continued)

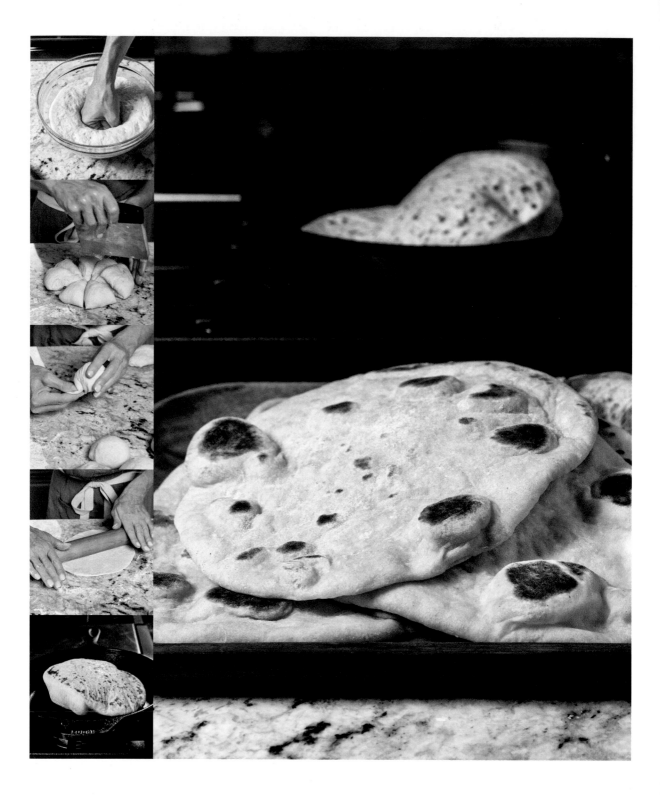

HOUSEMADE PITA *(continued)*

Punch the dough to knock it back, then remove from the bowl onto a lightly floured work surface. Briefly knead to form a ball and gently press down to form a thick disk. Using a bench scraper or chef's knife, cut the disk like a pizza into eight evenly sized wedges. Do not flour your work surface at this point; you'll need the countertop to slightly grip the dough to roll each wedge into a ball.

Working with one wedge at a time, with two hands, fold the dough toward the center and pinch in the middle, place the pinch side down on the countertop and move it in a circular motion, using one hand to form the ball. Place the dough ball to the side on your countertop and keep it covered with a clean kitchen towel. Repeat with the remaining seven wedges. Let set to rest for 10 minutes.

Working with one dough ball at a time, lightly dust your work surface with flour (you'll only need a little flour to prevent sticking) and roll the dough ball with a rolling pin to approximately 6½ inches (16.5 cm) in diameter, about ¼ inch (6 mm) thick. Place the dough disk onto a piece of parchment paper in a single layer (do not stack) and keep them covered with a clean kitchen towel to rest, 20 minutes.

Place a cast-iron skillet or griddle over medium heat for several minutes until well heated. Using heavy-duty paper towels, lightly wipe the skillet or griddle with safflower oil to thinly coat. When the pan is hot, place the dough disk, tacky side down first, into the pan. Cook until bubbles break the surface and it's lightly golden in spots on the bottom, about 45 seconds. Flip and toast until lightly golden in random spots and puffed like a pillow on the other side, about 30 seconds. Sometimes it puffs up a little or a lot, donta you worry! If it's golden in random spots, then remove it. Repeat with the rest and stack on top of each other.

Serve immediately or cool completely and then stack, with a small piece of parchment paper between each. Place the stack in a large zip-top bag and keep in the refrigerator for a couple of days, rewarming as needed, or freeze for up to 2 months.

PROVOLONE-STUFFED LONG HOTS

My good friend Chantal first introduced me to these. She often makes them for me because she knows I love hot peppers. I can eat them as is, with nothing else, one after the other. They're so good, so simple. Serve on the side with my Sunday Meat-a-ballz (page 54) and/or Homemade Marinara with Pasta from Scratch (page 83). It's Italian!

Makes 8 peppers

8 fresh Italian long hot peppers (fatter ones are better for stuffing)
3 tbsp (45 ml) olive oil
½ tsp kosher salt
Fresh finely ground black pepper
6 oz (170 g) wedge sharp provolone cheese

Preheat the oven to 400°F (200°C).

Cut a long slit, lengthwise, down the peppers. Run your index finger inside the slit to open it up slightly, forming a pocket.

Arrange the peppers on a rimmed baking sheet, evenly spacing them apart. Drizzle the oil over the peppers and season with the salt and a few turns from the pepper mill.

Place in the oven to roast until the peppers are tender, 8 to 12 minutes, depending on the size of the long hots.

Meanwhile, slice the cheese into ¼-inch (6-mm)-thick slices. Remove the peppers from the oven and evenly fill the pockets with the cheese, breaking the slices as needed to fit. Return the peppers to the oven and bake until the cheese melts, 2 to 4 minutes.

Serve immediately.

HEARTY CHICKEN TUSCAN ZUPPA

Zuppa, pronounced zùp-pa, means soup. It's Italian! This is a perfect lunch or starter for dinner, or you can load up your bowl and call it supper. I'm very picky when it comes to zuppa. You must start with good chicken stock—that's what makes it delicious and comforting—and adding the lacinato kale not only gives it great *flavah* but nutrition, too. Cooking dried cannellini beans in your pressure cooker is quick and easy (see the recipe in the headnote of the Sautéed Swiss Chard with Cannellini Beans on page 117). If you're using canned, 1 (15-ounce (425-g)) can equals 1¾ cups.

Makes 4 To 6 servings

1½–2 lbs (681–908 g) split bone-in, skin-on chicken breasts (organic preferred)

1 tbsp (15 ml) avocado oil

3 tsp (15 g) kosher salt, divided + more for seasoning the chicken

1¼ tsp (2 g) freshly ground black pepper, divided + more for seasoning the chicken

2 tbsp (30 ml) good-quality olive oil + more for serving

1 cup (160 g) diced onion

1 cup (128 g) peeled, ½-inch (1.3-cm) diced carrots

6–8 cups (1.4–1.9 L) chicken stock, preferably homemade (page 51)

Preheat the oven to 400°F (200°C).

Place the chicken breasts, skin side up, in a 9 x 12–inch (23 x 30–cm) baking dish. Drizzle the oil over the chicken skin and season with salt and pepper. Bake until just cooked through, 25 to 35 minutes. Remove the dish from the oven and let the chicken cool.

When the chicken is cool enough to handle, remove and discard the skin. Shred the chicken off the bones, reserving the bones (we'll need them later). Reserve 2 cups (280 g) of shredded chicken for the soup and refrigerate the remainder for lunch the next day, to make chicken salad, chicken quesadillas, as a topping on salads or whatever you like. Cover the chicken with plastic wrap to keep it moist as you prepare the soup.

Add the olive oil to a 6-quart (5.7-L) pot or Dutch oven over medium heat. Add the onion, carrots, ½ teaspoon of salt and ¼ teaspoon of pepper and sauté until the carrots are tender crisp, 3 to 4 minutes. Add 6 cups (1.4 L) of the stock and the reserved chicken bones; they'll help boost a little extra *flavah* in the stock. Season with 2 teaspoons (12 g) of salt and ¾ teaspoon of pepper and stir. Bring the stock to a gentle bubble over medium-high heat, then reduce to simmer. Cover and cook until the carrots soften, about 10 minutes.

(Continued)

1 cup (112 g) pipette pasta (for homemade, see Chefie Tip)

4–5 oz (113–142 g) Tuscan kale (also known as lacinato), stemmed and leaves torn (about 3 cups (55 g))

1¾ cups (315 g) cooked cannellini beans (if using canned, drained and rinsed)

⅓ cup (33 g) packed, freshly grated Parmigiano-Reggiano cheese + more for serving

1 loaf fresh ciabatta bread

Remove and discard the chicken bones. Bring the soup back to a bubble over medium-high heat, toss in the pasta and stir well, to prevent sticking. Immediately reduce to a simmer and cover. Cook until the pasta is al dente, about 10 minutes.

Add the kale, beans, ½ teaspoon of salt and ¼ teaspoon of pepper and stir. Simmer until the kale is wilted, 1 to 2 minutes, while stirring. Remove the pot from the heat, add the shredded chicken and Parmigiano-Reggiano cheese and stir. As the soup sets, the pasta will expand and absorb some of the stock, so if you'd like more stock, add the remaining 2 cups (480 ml), then season to taste.

Ladle among bowls. Drizzle with extra-virgin olive oil and grated Parmigiano-Reggiano cheese on top. Slice the ciabatta and pass around the table.

Chefie Tip:

For homemade pasta, follow my pasta from scratch recipe (page 86). Form walnut-sized pieces of the dough and extrude them through the large macaroni plate of a KitchenAid pasta press attachment into ¾-inch (2-cm) pieces; they'll bend naturally when cut. Lightly toss with flour and dry them out at room temperature to hold their shape. Cover and simmer the pasta in the soup, 5 to 6 minutes.

AVGOLÉMONO SOUP

Avgolémono is a broth thickened with eggs and spiked with lemons, used for sauces and soups. It's Greek! The first time I had this soup, I was nine months pregnant with my son, Costas; it was the blizzard of 2001 and my Greek neighbor, Aglaïa, made it for me. I immediately fell in love with it, then re-created my own version from my memory and have been making it for my Greek Cypriot family ever since. My son Costas is now 20 years old, so this recipe is a keeper. I've always used rice, but you could substitute orzo pasta, too.

Makes 8 to 10 servings

1 (4-lb (1.8-kg)) whole chicken, legs tied together

4–5 ribs celery with leaves, roughly chopped

4 carrots, unpeeled, tops trimmed and roughly chopped

1 large onion, peeled and chopped

5 fresh or 2 dry bay leaves

1 small bunch fresh thyme sprigs

1 small bunch Italian parsley with stems + 3 tbsp (11 g) chopped, for serving

1 tbsp (18 g) kosher salt + more to taste

½ tbsp (4 g) black peppercorns

1½ cups (300 g) long-grain white rice

Add the chicken, celery, carrots, onion, bay leaves, thyme, parsley bunch, salt and peppercorns to an 8-quart (7.6-L) stock pot. Pour 14 to 16 cups (3.4 to 3.8 L) of cold water into the pot and bring to a rapid bubble over high heat. Reduce to simmer and cook, uncovered, until the chicken is cooked through, about 1 hour. Skim and remove the foam as it rises to the surface while simmering.

Remove the chicken and set it aside to cool. Continue simmering the broth, covered, while the chicken cools for 15 to 20 minutes. When the chicken is cool enough to handle, shred the meat off the bones and return the bones to the broth, discarding the skin. Cover and refrigerate the chicken; you'll have about 3½ cups (500 g). Continue simmering the broth, covered, for 3 hours. Remove the chicken from the fridge 30 minutes before finishing the soup, to remove the chill.

Remove the pot from the heat and let it cool slightly. Drain into a colander fitted over a large bowl to catch the stock. Push on the solids to squeeze out the stock. You should have about 3 quarts (2.8 L) of stock. Return the stock to the pot and season vigorously to taste with kosher salt. This is a very important step to ensure a flavorful soup.

Bring the stock to a bubble over high heat, add the rice and stir. Reduce to a simmer, cover and cook until the rice is al dente, 10 to 12 minutes.

(Continued)

AVGOLÉMONO SOUP *(continued)*

4 large eggs, at room temperature

½ cup (120 ml) freshly squeezed lemon juice (from about 3 large lemons)

Greek olive oil or extra-virgin olive oil, for serving

Freshly cracked black pepper, for serving

Whisk the eggs in a medium bowl, then slowly drizzle two to three ladles of hot broth, a little at a time, into the bowl with the eggs while rapidly and constantly whisking. Slowly pour the tempered eggs into the soup, while whisking constantly. Heat over medium-low and cook until the eggs slightly thicken the soup, 2 to 5 minutes, whisking periodically. The soup will continue to thicken as it sets, donta you worry!

Remove the pot from the heat and stir in the shredded chicken and lemon juice until warmed through. Let stand to further thicken and build flavor, about 20 minutes. The longer it sets, the better it gets and the thicker it gets. Season to taste with kosher salt. Divide among bowls, drizzle a little Greek or extra-virgin olive oil over the top and garnish with black pepper and chopped parsley, because you're fancy!

Chefie Tip:
Freeze leftover soup in clear, plastic, quart-sized (1-L) containers with tight-fitting lids for up to 2 months. Thaw and rewarm when ready to eat. Soup that has been frozen may need some more stock when reheating as the rice absorbs the stock.

PASTA E FAGIOLI NAPOLETANA

My Italian–American father called this pasta fasul. It means pasta and beans. It was the first dish I ever prepared for my husband (then boyfriend). There's something to be said about the saying, "The way to someone's heart is through their stomach." Cooking cannellini beans in your pressure cooker is quick, easy and makes them taste amazing (see the recipe in the intro in the Sautéed Swiss Chard with Cannellini Beans recipe on page 117). If you're using canned, you will need 1½ (15-ounce (425-g)) cans to equal the 2½ cups needed for this recipe.

Makes 6 servings

2 tbsp (30 ml) olive oil

1 cup (128 g) peeled, ½-inch (1.3-cm) diced carrots (2 large)

1 cup (160 g) diced onion (1 medium onion)

2 tsp (12 g) kosher salt, divided

¾ tsp fresh ground black pepper, divided

4 cloves garlic, minced

2 tsp (1 g) minced fresh rosemary

¼ tsp red pepper flakes + more for serving

4 cups (960 ml) chicken stock, preferably homemade (page 51)

1 (½-lb (227-g)) wedge Parmigiano-Reggiano, with rind

1 (28-oz (794-g)) can whole peeled San Marzano tomatoes

⅔ cup (75 g) ditalini pasta (for homemade, see Chefie Tip)

Add the oil to a 6-quart (5.7-L) pot or Dutch oven over medium heat. Add the carrots, onion, ½ teaspoon of salt and ¼ teaspoon of pepper and sauté until tender, yet still crisp, 3 to 4 minutes.

Add the garlic, rosemary and red pepper flakes and sauté until the *gálick* is fragrant, about 1 minute. Add the chicken stock, then cut the rind off of the Parmigiano-Reggiano wedge and toss it into the soup.

Drain the San Marzano tomatoes over a bowl. Place the tomatoes into a medium bowl and crush the tomatoes with your hands, don't be a wimp! Add the tomatoes into the pot and fill the can one-quarter of the way with cold water, then gently swirl the can to release the tomato juices from the walls of the can and add the water with juices into the pot. You can save the tomato purée to make tomato soup, Bloody Marys or homemade barbecue sauce, if you like.

Season the soup with 1½ teaspoons (9 g) of salt and ½ teaspoon of pepper and stir well. Bring to a gentle bubble over medium-high heat. Reduce to a simmer and cook until the flavors build, 20 minutes. Add the pasta and stir. Reduce to a simmer, cover and cook the pasta until al dente, 16 to 18 minutes, stirring two times. Don't let the pasta stick.

(Continued)

PASTA E FAGIOLI NAPOLETANA *(continued)*

2½ cups (450 g) cooked cannellini beans (if using canned, drained and rinsed), divided

Good-quality extra-virgin olive oil

½ cup (20 g) sliced fresh basil

Smash 1 cup (180 g) of the beans in a medium bowl, using a potato masher or the back of a fork, until finely mashed; this helps thicken the soup. Add the mashed beans and the remaining beans and warm through, about 2 minutes. If you used canned beans, cover and keep the leftover beans in the refrigerator to toss on salads or sautéed greens.

Remove the soup from the heat and discard the cheese rind. Season to taste. Divide the soup among bowls. Drizzle with extra-virgin olive oil and grate Parmigiano-Reggiano on top. Garnish with basil and red pepper flakes. Serve immediately.

Chefie Tip:

For homemade pasta, follow my pasta from scratch recipe (page 86). Form walnut-sized pieces of the dough and extrude them through the large macaroni plate of a KitchenAid pasta press attachment into ½-inch (1.3-cm) pieces. Lightly toss with flour and dry them out at room temperature to hold their shape. Cover and simmer the pasta in the soup, 5 to 6 minutes.

ROASTED PUMPKIN BISQUE

This soup is legit! It's incredibly easy to roast a pumpkin, and it makes this bisque restaurant worthy! I encourage you to make homemade chicken stock; it's better! I make this Roasted Pumpkin Bisque every Halloween; it's our family tradition.

Makes 8 servings

1 (4 lb (1.8-kg)) sugar pumpkin or pie pumpkin

Avocado oil

¼ cup (½ stick (56 g)) unsalted butter

1 cup (160 g) diced onion

1 cup (128 g) peeled, diced carrots

1 cup (101 g) diced celery ribs

2¼ tsp (11 g) kosher salt, divided + more for serving

¾ tsp fresh finely ground black pepper, divided + more for serving

½ cup (120 ml) good-quality white wine

4 cups (960 ml) chicken stock, preferably homemade (page 51) + more to thin, as necessary

¼ cup (55 g) packed dark brown sugar

3 tbsp (45 ml) honey

¼ tsp ground cloves

½–1 cup (120–240 ml) heavy cream, at room temperature + more for serving

Chives, snipped

Preheat the oven to 400°F (200°C). Line a baking sheet with parchment paper.

Remove the stem from the pumpkin and cut it in half, lengthwise, scraping out the insides, discarding the seeds (or keeping them to roast later).

Rub a little avocado oil over the pumpkin flesh and place the halves, flesh side down onto the parchment-lined baking sheet. Roast until fork-tender, 35 to 45 minutes. Remove the baking sheet from the oven and let the pumpkin cool. Pull away and discard the skin, mashing the pumpkin with a fork (see Chefie Tips). Set aside.

Melt the butter in a 6-quart (5.7-L) heavy-bottomed pot over medium heat. Toss in the onion, carrots and celery and season with ¾ teaspoon of salt and ¼ teaspoon of pepper. Sauté until tender, 7 to 8 minutes.

Deglaze the pot with the wine and reduce by half, about 1 minute. Add the stock, 3 to 3½ cups (735 to 860 g) of the mashed pumpkin, brown *shugá*, honey, ground cloves, 1½ teaspoons (9 g) of salt and ½ teaspoon of pepper. Stir. Bring to just under a bubble over medium-high heat, then reduce the heat to medium-low and continue to cook until the flavors combine, 25 to 30 minutes, stirring periodically.

(Continued)

ROASTED PUMPKIN BISQUE *(continued)*

Working in two batches, transfer the pumpkin soup mixture to a blender, and purée until smooth. Make sure to hold a kitchen towel over the lid of the blender while puréeing or the heat will blow off the top! Return the bisque to the pot, add the heavy cream as desired, and stir until warmed through over low heat. Add additional stock to thin the bisque, as needed. Season to taste with salt and pepper.

Divide the bisque among bowls and swirl a little extra heavy cream on top. Garnish with the chopped chives because you're fancy!

Chefie Tips:
You can make this 1 day ahead and refrigerate. Rewarm when you're ready to serve and thin with extra chicken stock, as needed.

If you want to roast some extra pumpkin to use for baking pie or bread or any other dessert, purée the roasted pumpkin in a food processor until smooth and if the purée seems watery line a large bowl with cheesecloth and place the purée in the cheesecloth. Twist and wring out the excess moisture, making a purse.

HOMEMADE CAESAR SALAD *with* GARLIC CROUTONS

Yasss! We're makin' homemade mayonnaise; it only takes 3 minutes in a food processor and is so much better than store-bought! I'm having you make a little more than you'll need for this recipe, so you can keep it in your refrigerator to smear on sandwiches all week long. Making the croutons, mayonnaise and dressing a few days ahead will make this recipe super easy to toss together à la minute.

Makes 4 servings

FOR THE HOMEMADE MAYONNAISE

3 large egg yolks, at room temperature

1½ tsp (8 ml) Dijon mustard

1 cup (240 ml) canola, safflower or avocado oil

2 tbsp (30 ml) freshly squeezed lemon juice

1 tbsp (15 ml) white distilled vinegar

1 tsp kosher salt

To make the mayonnaise, add the egg yolks and Dijon to a food processor fitted with the steel blade attachment and the emulsification insert (with the pin hole insert), through the feed tube.

Mix on high while slowly streaming the oil through the feed tube, a little at a time, so it slowly drizzles in. It'll take about 2 minutes and 30 seconds to add all the oil. If you don't have this insert, donta you worry! You can very slowly drizzle the oil through the feed tube or use a squeeze bottle for better control. Your texture should be just like a thick, creamy mayonnaise. The slower the drizzle, the thicker it'll be. If it's not thick and creamy, the dressing will be too thin and will not evenly coat the romaine. So, thin drizzle, very slow or even add in small droplets. Don't disappoint me!

Remove the lid of the food processor, add the lemon juice, vinegar and salt and blend on high speed for a few seconds to combine. Remove the mayo, leaving ½ cup (120 ml) in the food processor. Store the rest of the mayo in a container with a tight-fitting lid in your refrigerator. Use within a week.

(Continued)

HOMEMADE CAESAR SALAD *with* GARLIC CROUTONS *(continued)*

FOR THE SALAD

¼ cup (60 ml) freshly squeezed lemon juice (from about 2 lemons)

2 tbsp (30 ml) good-quality extra-virgin olive oil

2–4 anchovies, packed in oil, drained

Kosher salt + fresh finely ground black pepper

⅓ cup (33 g) packed, freshly grated Parmigiano-Reggiano + shavings for garnish

3 small–medium heads romaine lettuce, washed, dried, cored and sliced into 1-inch (2.5-cm) pieces

FOR THE GARLIC CROUTONS

½ cup (112 g) unsalted butter

⅓ cup (80 ml) olive oil

2 tbsp (4 g) roughly chopped fresh thyme leaves

1 (10–12-oz [283–340-g]) loaf day-old French baguette, ½-inch (1.3-cm) dice

1 tsp garlic powder

¾ tsp kosher salt

Fresh finely ground black pepper

To make the salad dressing, in the same food processor fitted with the steel blade attachment, add the lemon juice, olive oil and two anchovies to the ½ cup (120 ml) of mayo. Season with salt and pepper and give it a zip on high speed until the anchovies are finely minced and smooth, about 10 seconds. Taste the dressing; if you'd like more umami flavor, add one to two more anchovies and mix for several seconds until fully blended. Stir in the Parmigiano-Reggiano. As the dressing sets, it'll thicken.

To make the croutons, preheat the oven to 375°F (190°C). Melt the butter in a small saucepan over low heat, then remove the saucepan from the heat, pour in the olive oil and add the thyme. Stir. Toss the bread cubes in a large bowl with the butter/oil mixture until evenly coated. Sprinkle the garlic powder and the salt evenly over the bread cubes and toss.

Arrange the bread cubes evenly on a rimmed baking sheet. Freshly crack black pepper over them and bake until toasted and lightly golden, 14 to 18 minutes, tossing halfway through the bake time. Remove the baking sheet from the oven, toss the bread cubes and let them cool.

To assemble the salad, toss the romaine with ⅔ cup (160 ml) of the dressing in a large mixing bowl until evenly coated. Divide among four plates, garnish with shaved Parmigiano-Reggiano on top and top with the desired amount of croutons. Warning: These are addicting! Serve the remaining dressing on the side, to pass around.

SHANGHAI CHICKEN SALAD *with* SESAME GINGER VINAIGRETTE

This isn't an ordinary salad! Roasting your own chicken is juicier, and when it's bathed in this amazing vinaigrette it is insane! Slicing your own cabbage and carrots keeps them moist, fresh and crisp, so don't be lazy. Can't find Chinese (Napa) cabbage? Savoy is a great substitute; it's slightly sweeter than green cabbage. Serve this as a starter to stir-fried Asian noodles or enjoy for lunch with a glass of Riesling. You need this in your life, pronto!

Makes 4 servings

FOR THE CHICKEN

2 lbs (908 g) bone-in split, skin-on chicken breasts (about 2 breasts, organic preferred)

1½ tbsp (23 ml) avocado oil

1½ tsp (9 g) kosher salt

½ tsp fresh finely ground black pepper

Preheat the oven to 400°F (200°C).

To roast the chicken, place the chicken breasts, skin side up, in a 9 x 12 x 2–inch (23 x 30 x 5–cm) baking dish and drizzle the oil over the skin. Season with the salt and the pepper on both sides. Roast the chicken until juicy and just cooked through, 25 to 30 minutes. Remove the chicken from the pan and let it rest on a plate, about 10 minutes.

When the chicken is cool enough to handle, shred the meat off the bones into thin, long, bite-sized pieces, discarding the skin. You can save the bones (along with another chicken carcass) for making chicken stock, if you desire. They freeze great in a large zip-top bag.

(Continued)

SHANGHAI CHICKEN SALAD *with* SESAME GINGER VINAIGRETTE *(continued)*

FOR THE SESAME GINGER VINAIGRETTE

¼ cup (4 g) chopped cilantro, divided

¼ cup (60 ml) champagne vinegar

¼ cup (60 ml) toasted pure sesame oil

3 tbsp (45 g) sugar

2 tbsp (12 g) finely grated peeled ginger (see Chefie Tips)

2 tbsp (30 ml) avocado oil

1½ tbsp (23 ml) less-sodium soy sauce

Zest of 1 lime

2 tbsp (30 ml) freshly squeezed lime juice

1½ tsp (7 g) kosher salt, divided

¼ tsp fresh finely ground black pepper

FOR THE SALAD

½ medium–large head Napa or Savoy cabbage

1 cup (110 g) shredded carrots

3 green onions, thinly sliced on an angle (using the entire onion)

½ cup (8 g) chopped cilantro

¾ tsp kosher salt

¼ tsp fresh finely ground black pepper

3 tsp (10 g) sesame seeds, toasted (see Chefie Tips)

1 cup (45 g) chow mein noodles

Meanwhile, to make the vinaigrette, whisk the cilantro with the vinegar, sesame oil, *shugá*, ginger, avocado oil, soy sauce, lime zest and juice, ¾ teaspoon of salt and ¼ teaspoon of pepper in an extra large bowl. Toss the shredded chicken into the bowl and season with an additional ¾ teaspoon of salt. Toss. Let sit to marinate, 5 to 10 minutes.

To make the salad, remove the outer leaves and core from the cabbage and discard. Thinly slice the cabbage into long strands, making 6 cups (420 g). Add the cabbage, carrots, green onions, cilantro, salt and pepper to the bowl with the chicken. Toss well to evenly coat all the ingredients with the vinaigrette. Season to taste. Don't let the salad sit longer than a couple minutes, it'll get soggy.

Divide and pile the salad high among four plates or on a large serving platter. Garnish with the sesame seeds and chow mein noodles. Serve immediately. Don't forget the chopsticks!

Chefie Tips:

Toasting the sesame seeds is optional but worth it. Toss them in a small skillet over medium-low heat briefly, while constantly swirling the pan to release the natural oils from the seeds, warming them through.

Using a microplane works best when finely grating the ginger. You'll need a good amount, so grab a nice-sized hand of ginger (a 5- to 6-inch (13- to 15-cm) piece) at the market.

BALELA SALAD

Balela is a Middle Eastern bean salad made with chickpeas and black beans. I tweaked mine a bit and added quinoa for some grain. It's the perfect beefy lunch without the meat. You can also enjoy it wrapped with my Housemade Pita (page 23) with tzatziki (page 58), drizzled with tahini or paired with grilled chicken or fish. Here's the deal, I love dried beans, freshly cooked: There are no preservatives and you can add whichever aromatics you like while cooking to boost the *flavah*. I cook 'em in my pressure cooker (see the recipe in the headnote of the Sautéed Swiss Chard with Cannellini Beans on page 117) because it's quick and easy, but if you forget to soak them ahead sub in canned, drained and rinsed. Oh! If cooking the dried beans for this recipe, do each type separately; the color from the black beans will bleed onto the chickpeas if they are cooked together and their cook times are different (see Chefie Tip).

Makes 4 To 6 servings

½ cup (85 g) quinoa

1½ tsp (7 g) kosher salt, divided + a pinch for the quinoa

3 tbsp (45 ml) good-quality extra-virgin olive oil

Zest of 1 large lemon

3 tbsp (45 ml) lemon juice

2 tbsp (20 g) finely minced shallots

½ tsp fresh finely ground black pepper, divided

1¾ cups (425 g) cooked chickpeas (if using canned, drained and rinsed)

1¾ cups (425 g) cooked black beans (if using canned, drained and rinsed)

1½ cups (225 g) halved cherry or grape tomatoes

½ cup (30 g) chopped Italian parsley

¼ cup (23 g) chopped mint

Rinse the quinoa in a fine-mesh strainer and place into a 2-quart (1.9-L) saucepan. Add 1 cup (240 ml) of cold water and a pinch of salt and stir. Bring to a bubble over high heat. Reduce to a simmer and cover until the liquid is almost absorbed and the quinoa is tender, yet still chewy, about 12 minutes. Remove the pan from the heat, fluff the quinoa with a fork, strain it in a fine-mesh strainer and immediately rinse under cold water to stop the cooking and cool the grains, draining completely. Using a rubber spatula, press and squeeze out as much of the excess moisture as you can.

Meanwhile, in a large bowl, whisk the olive oil, lemon zest, lemon juice, shallots, ½ teaspoon of salt and ¼ teaspoon of pepper until combined. Add the chickpeas, black beans, cherry tomatoes, quinoa, 1 teaspoon of salt, ¼ teaspoon of pepper, parsley and mint to the bowl and toss well until combined with the vinaigrette.

You can make this up to several hours ahead and keep at room temperature, covered, or refrigerate overnight. If making ahead, let the salad come to room temperature for about 30 minutes before serving to remove the chill.

Chefie Tip:
If using presoaked dried beans in a pressure cooker, cook times are about 10 minutes for black beans and about 25 minutes for chickpeas. Use the quick-release method.

GRUYÈRE *and* THYME POPOVERS

These popovers were inspired by my good friend Jeannette. I added thyme,
Gruyère and fleur del sel butter to be fancy. They're basically Yorkshire pudding
(a traditional English dish served with meats and gravy), but I added a little pizzaz,
I can't help myself. Serve with whatever you want: soup, salad, fish,
meat or chicken, there're no rules here!

If you don't have a popover pan, you can make these in a cupcake/muffin tin, but a
popover pan makes these puff even higher, making them legit.

Makes 6 servings

3 large eggs

1 cup (240 ml) whole milk

½ tsp kosher salt

1 cup (125 g) all-purpose flour

3 tsp (12 g) vegetable
shortening, divided

⅓ cup (26 g) freshly grated
Gruyère, chilled

3 tsp (2 g) fresh thyme leaves

6 tbsp (84 g) unsalted butter,
at room temperature

Fleur de sel

Whisk the eggs, milk and salt until combined. Sift the flour into
the milk mixture and whisk until smooth, about 1 minute. The
batter will be thin, donta you worry! Let it rest for 10 minutes, to
relax the gluten.

Adjust your oven rack to the middle position and preheat
the oven to 425°F (220°C). When the oven is heated, add
½ teaspoon of shortening to the bottom of each cup of a six-
cup popover pan. Place the pan in the oven until the shortening
melts and is hot, 3 to 5 minutes. Be careful removing the pan.
Divide the batter among the six cups, filling each halfway. Add
approximately 1 tablespoon (4 g) of grated Gruyère and ½ teaspoon
of thyme leaves to each cup and briefly stir with the back of a
spoon to push the Gruyère and thyme into the batter.

Bake until puffed and lightly golden brown, about 15 minutes.
Reduce the oven temperature to 300°F (150°C), to control the
browning and further cook the inside, about 5 more minutes. Do
NOT open the oven door or the popovers will deflate!

Serve warm with the butter in a ramekin, lightly sprinkled with
fleur de sel for spreading. You know why (wink)!

HOMEMADE CHICKEN STOCK *Two Ways*

Technically this is not a starter but it is the start to a good soup or sauce.

Any time you roast a whole chicken, save the carcass; it's not trash, it's treasure! Place the carcass in a large zip-top bag and refrigerate for up to 2 days or freeze up to 2 months, until you're ready to make stock. Make homemade chicken stock—it's easy and BETTER than store-bought! In fact, do a taste test, side by side. I'll say no more. Here, I even give you two different ways to prepare it. SO easy!

Makes 3 quarts (2.8 L)

1 whole chicken carcass

4–5 celery ribs with leaves, roughly chopped

4 carrots, tops trimmed, unpeeled and roughly chopped

1 large onion, peeled and chopped

5 fresh or 2 dried bay leaves

1 small bunch fresh thyme sprigs

1 small bunch Italian parsley with stems

1 tbsp (18 g) kosher salt + more for seasoning

½ tbsp (4 g) black peppercorns

On the Stovetop: Add the chicken carcass, celery, carrots, onion, bay leaves, thyme, parsley, salt and peppercorns to an 8-quart (7.6-L) stock pot. Pour 14 to 16 cups (3.4 to 3.8 L) of cold water into the pot and bring to a rapid bubble over high heat. Reduce to a simmer and cover for 4 hours. Skim and remove the foam as it rises to the surface while simmering, periodically, as needed.

Remove the pot from the heat and let the stock cool slightly. Drain into a colander fitted over a large bowl to catch the stock. Push on the solids to squeeze out the stock. Season to taste with kosher salt. Cool completely before storing.

In a Pressure Cooker: Add the chicken carcass, celery, carrots, onion, bay leaves, thyme, parsley, salt and peppercorns to a 6- to 8-quart (5.7- to 7.5-L) pressure cooker insert pot. Pour cold water into the pot, to fill to the two-thirds line marked inside the pot. Do not exceed the two-thirds line inside the pot. Pressure cook on HIGH for 1½ hours. Use the natural release.

Let the stock cool slightly. Drain into a colander fitted over a large bowl to catch the stock. Push on the solids to squeeze out the stock. Season to taste with kosher salt. Cool completely before storing.

Refrigerate the stock in tight-fitting, quart-sized (1-L) clear containers for several hours to overnight, then skim and remove any fat congealed at the top. Refrigerate for up to several days or freeze for up to a few months.

ROCKSTAR DINNERS

Don't be intimidated at the thought of cooking from scratch. It's not hard—it's empowering! You can do it! It builds your confidence and strengthens your mind to know you can accomplish anything. Plus, it's damn delicious.

Sunday Meat-a-ballz (page 54) are not just for Sunday—if you want them on Tuesday, do it! Using a pressure cooker speeds up the time considerably and results in incredibly tender and flavorful meat-a-ballz. Or cook hands-free in your slow cooker with my easy Homemade Marinara (page 83).

Using your pressure cooker or slow cooker as your sous chef will also help you prepare the Chilaquiles Verdes con Pollo (page 61) and Indoor Barbecued Pulled Pork with Honey Coleslaw (page 69) without compromising the *flavah*. In some instances, it's *bettah!*

Grilling vegetables and proteins is quick and imparts so much flavor! If it's the middle of winter and your grill is covered in snow, don't despair. When you have a hankering for Grilled Chicken Gyros (page 58), a cast-iron grill pan is a golden replacement and mimics the char flavor of a gas grill, plus gives you more grilling control. It creates beautiful grill marks, too. A food styling secret weapon. That's our little secret!

SUNDAY MEAT-A-BALLZ

These are not meatballs, they're meat-a-ballz! That's how my Nana said it. The keys to a good meat-a-ball are getting the size right and making sure to pan-fry them. These have the perfect ratio of crispy exterior and tender interior. I love to make these all year long, even at the beach. I wake up early, fry 'em and toss 'em in my Homemade Marinara (page 83; don't disappoint me, make it homemade!), then place them in my slow cooker and head out for the day. When we return and open the door, we're immediately met with the aroma that says, "Welcome home!" Nothin' *bettah!*

Makes 6 servings

1½ lbs (681 g) ground beef, veal and pork mixture

⅓ cup (70 g) grated Spanish onion

⅓ cup (17 g) finely chopped fresh Italian parsley

¼ cup (27 g) seasoned Italian breadcrumbs

2 tbsp (32 g) tomato paste

1 large egg, whisked

1½ tsp (3 g) granulated garlic

1½ tsp (7 g) kosher salt + more for seasoning

¾ tsp fresh finely ground black pepper

1½ cups (360 ml) canola oil

4½–5 cups (1.1–1.2 L) Homemade Marinara (page 83)

Add the ground meat, onion, parsley, breadcrumbs, tomato paste, egg, granulated garlic, salt and pepper to a large bowl. Gently mix with clean hands until combined. Don't be a wimp! Using a medium cookie scoop or tablespoon (measuring approximately 2 tablespoons [30 g]), form the meat mixture into medium-sized balls. Place the balls on a plate; the mixture should make 28 to 30 meat-a-ballz.

Place a 12-inch (30-cm) frying pan over medium heat and add the oil. When the oil is heated and shimmers, add half of the meat-a-ballz (about 15) and pan-fry until browned, about 2 minutes on each side (4 minutes total). Remove the meat-a-ballz, using a slotted spoon, to a paper towel–lined plate. Lightly sprinkle with salt. Repeat the process with the second batch.

Meanwhile, add the marinara sauce to a 6-quart (5.7-L) heavy-bottomed pot over medium heat and let it come to a gentle bubble. Reduce the heat to simmer. Gently stir in the meat-a-ballz. Don't break the balls! Cover and simmer until the meat-a-ballz are uber tender, 45 to 55 minutes, gently stirring periodically. The beef needs a long braise to become very tender.

You can also add the fried meat-a-ballz and marinara to a slow cooker on high for 2 hours or low for 4 hours, or in a pressure cooker on high for 25 minutes. Remove the lid and continue cooking to reduce any accumulated steaming liquid, if needed, 5 to 10 minutes.

Chefie Tip:
The best way to dispose of the oil is to let it cool completely, add it to a large zip-top bag, zip closed and place in the trash.

JAMAICAN JERK STEAK

This is my favorite go-to steak to make. It's easy, insanely delicious and everyone loves it! The fat from the skirt steak balances the spice perfectly in this dish. If you want to use this jerk rub on chicken, I've found it's better to reduce the chiles to only one small, seeded Scotch bonnet or habanero chile, so it's not too overpowering.

Makes 4 servings

3 small Scotch bonnet peppers, stemmed and chopped (can substitute with habanero chiles)

4–5 green onions, sliced, whites and dark green separated

⅓ cup (80 ml) olive oil

⅓ cup (73 g) packed light brown sugar

2 tsp (3 g) granulated garlic powder

2 tsp (4 g) ground allspice

2 tsp (5 g) ground cinnamon

½ tsp ground cloves

½ tsp freshly grated nutmeg

2 skirt steaks (1½ lbs (681 g) total)

3 tsp (14 g) kosher salt

¾ tsp fresh finely ground black pepper

Purée the peppers and the whites of the green onions with the oil in a mini food processor or mini blender, fitted with the steel blade, until smooth with a few chunks left. Pour the pepper oil into a medium bowl and add the brown *shugá*, garlic powder, allspice, cinnamon, cloves and nutmeg and mix well, using a fork, making a wet paste.

Slather the paste over the steaks on both sides. Cover and marinate in the refrigerator, 2 to 4 hours. Remove the steaks from the refrigerator and let them come to room temperature 30 minutes before grilling.

Place a grill or cast-iron grill pan over medium heat. Flick off any chiles or onion bits, leaving the rub and season both steaks with the salt and pepper on both sides. Grill the steaks, about 2 minutes on each side, with the lid up, for medium-rare doneness. Remove the steaks from the grill and let them rest, 8 minutes.

Cut both steaks in half, crosswise, then slice each half lengthwise against the grain into thin slices. Arrange on a small platter and garnish with the dark green onion slices.

GRILLED CHICKEN GYROS

Be authentic: It's pronounced *yíros* not *j-eye-ros*. The g is silent and you roll the r. Traditionally, gyros are made with meat that's cooked on a vertical spit, but pork and chicken are very common, too. Don't freak out at the thought of making housemade pita, it's easier than you think and tastes freakin' insane! If substituting store-bought pita, pocketless is better here.

Makes 5 servings

FOR THE GYROS

1½ lbs (681 g) boneless skinless chicken breasts (organic preferred)

⅓ cup (80 ml) olive oil

2 cloves garlic, finely grated

Zest of 1 lemon

5 Housemade Pitas (page 23)

1¼ tsp (6 g) kosher salt + more for seasoning the tomato

½ tsp fresh finely ground black pepper + more for seasoning the tomato

1 large ripe tomato, diced

FOR THE TZATZIKI

1 clove garlic

1 tbsp (15 ml) freshly squeezed lemon juice

1 (7-oz (198-g)) container 2% or 5% low-fat Greek yogurt

¼ of a hothouse cucumber, peeled, seeded and grated (to equal ⅓ cup (62 g))

2 tbsp (7 g) chopped dill + more for garnish

½ tsp kosher salt

⅛ tsp cayenne

½ of a small red onion, thinly sliced, to serve (see Chefie Tip on page 62)

First, we marinate the chicken: Place the chicken in a large zip-top bag, pushing out all the air and zip closed. Pound the chicken breasts to even thickness, using the flat side of a meat mallet. Unzip the bag and add the olive oil, *gálick* and lemon zest. Massage the chicken to evenly coat and cover. Zip closed and marinate for up to 4 hours in the refrigerator. This is a good time to make the pita. Then remove the chicken and let it sit at room temperature 20 to 25 minutes before cooking. Preheat the oven to 350°F (175°C) and heat your grill or grill pan over medium heat. Stack and fully wrap the pita in aluminum foil and place into the oven, to warm through, about 15 minutes, as needed.

Season the chicken with the salt and pepper on both sides. When the grill is fully heated, grill the chicken until cooked through and juicy, 4 to 5 minutes on each side. Don't overcook it! It'll be dry. Remove the chicken from the grill and place it on a cutting board to rest for 8 minutes. Then thinly slice the chicken.

Meanwhile, toss and season the tomato with salt and pepper in a small bowl and set aside.

To make the tzatziki, in a medium bowl, finely grate the garlic, add the lemon juice and stir. It mellows the *gálick*. Add the yogurt, grated cucumber, dill, salt and cayenne and stir well until combined.

To assemble, divide the chicken among the five pitas, topping half of each pita. Slather a generous amount of tzatziki over the chicken and top with desired amount of tomatoes and onion. Garnish with dill and fold in half to close. Serve immediately or wrap in foil and keep warm for up to 15 minutes.

CHILAQUILES VERDES con POLLO

Chilaquiles verdes con pollo: Clearly . . . it's Mexican! This is the ultimate Mexican comfort food and it's my absolute favorite! The flavors are fresh, bright, bold and spicy. Deflaming the onion, as mentioned in my Chefie Tips, is something I learned from Chef Rick Bayless—it's a golden tip. Cubanelle peppers may not be traditional but I like their slight sweetness here, balancing the spiciness from the chiles in the sauce. You can also place this in a slow cooker on high for 2 hours or low for 4 to 6 hours after you have puréed the salsa verde and browned the chicken.

Makes 5 to 6 servings

10 tomatillos, stemmed, husked and rinsed

4 Cubanelle peppers

2 poblano chiles

2 Serrano chiles (optional; if you like it spicy), divided

4½ tbsp (68 ml) avocado oil, divided

1¼ tsp (6 g) kosher salt + more for seasoning the peppers

½ tsp fresh finely ground black pepper + more for seasoning the peppers

6 cloves garlic, sliced

5 green onions, sliced, whites and dark greens separated

2 cups (480 ml) chicken stock, preferably homemade (page 51)

Adjust your oven rack directly under the broiler and preheat the broiler on high.

Place the tomatillos, Cubanelle peppers, poblano chiles and 1 Serrano chile (if using) onto a foil-lined, rimmed baking sheet and rub ½ tablespoon (8 ml) of oil evenly over all the tomatillos, peppers and chiles. Season with salt and pepper and place under the broiler until tender and nicely charred on both sides, 6 to 9 minutes, flipping halfway through. Remove the peppers from the oven and let them rest until they are cool enough to handle. Remove all the stems and seeds from the peppers. This will remove the bitterness. I'm obsessed with spicy foods, but I've found when I left the seeds from the poblano and Serrano chiles, the spice took over too much. Remove as desired to your liking.

Adjust the oven rack to the middle position and preheat the oven to 400°F (200°C). Place a 6-quart (5.7-L) Dutch oven over medium heat. Add 2 tablespoons (30 ml) of oil and when the oil is heated, add the garlic and the whites of the green onions. Season with a pinch of salt and pepper and sauté until the *gálick* is fragrant, 1 to 2 minutes. Add the onion mixture to a blender and set the pot aside for the chicken.

Place the tomatillos, peppers, chiles and chicken stock into the blender with the garlic and onion. Purée until smooth. Season to taste and set aside. It'll yield about 5 cups (1.2 kg).

(Continued)

CHILAQUILES VERDES *con* POLLO *(continued)*

2¼–2½ lbs (1–1.1 kg) boneless, skinless chicken thighs (organic preferred)

1½ tsp (4 g) ground cumin

1½ tsp (4 g) ground coriander

Fried Corn Tortilla Chips (page 12)

2 limes, 1 cut in half, 1 cut into wedges

½ lb (227 g) grated Pepper Jack or Monterey Jack cheese (see Chefie Tips)

1 small red or white onion, thinly sliced (see Chefie Tips)

Mexican crema or sour cream

½ cup (8 g) lightly chopped cilantro

Pat the chicken dry and season with the 1¼ teaspoons salt and ½ teaspoon pepper on both sides. Place the reserved pot over medium to medium-high heat. Add 1 to 2 tablespoons (15 to 30 ml) of the oil. When the oil is heated and shimmers, add the chicken in one layer. Sear both sides until golden brown, about 2 minutes per side, working in two batches, if all of the chicken does not comfortably fit. Drain off the excess fat in the pot, leaving the chicken.

Pour the salsa verde over the chicken, add the cumin and coriander and stir. Cover and place in the oven until the chicken is fork tender, about 45 minutes. This is a great time to fry the tortilla chips.

Remove the pot from the oven and let the chicken rest, about 10 minutes. Using two forks, shred the chicken in the salsa verde, freshly squeeze one lime into the sauce and stir. Season to taste.

Coarsely crumble a couple handfuls of the tortilla chips and place in the bottom of a shallow bowl. Ladle the chicken and salsa verde over the chips. Divide and sprinkle the cheese on top; the heat of the sauce will melt the cheese. Repeat with the remaining bowls.

Slice the remaining Serrano chile, if using. Garnish each bowl with the sliced Serrano chile, green onions, onion slices, a dollop of crema or sour cream and cilantro, because you're fancy! Serve with lime wedges on the side for squeezing.

Chefie Tips:

Deflame the onion by soaking the slices in cold water for 10 to 15 minutes while cooking the chicken. Drain before garnishing.

Leave the grated cheese at room temperature, so it melts faster when topping.

CHICKEN SATAY *with* PEANUT SAUCE

This is my daughter Isabella's favorite! This sauce is so freakin' good. If you have any left over, rewarm and toss it with cooked lo mein noodles, udon, soba, even fettuccine the next day for lunch or dinner, garnished with chopped cilantro and peanuts. You can thin out the reheated sauce with some of the pasta water. You're welcome. Take this to work the next day for lunch and you'll be the envy of the office.

Makes 8 to 12 servings as an appetizer or 4 to 5 servings for dinner, served with coconut rice

FOR THE SATAY

½ cup (120 ml) peanut oil

¼ cup (60 ml) less-sodium soy sauce

1 tbsp (15 g) sugar

1 tbsp (6 g) grated, peeled ginger root

2 large cloves garlic, grated

1 lime, zested

2 lbs (908 g) chicken tenders sliced in half lengthwise

FOR THE PEANUT SAUCE

1 tbsp (15 ml) peanut oil

1 clove garlic, minced

1 tbsp (6 g) minced, peeled ginger root

1–2 fresh or dried Thai bird's eye chiles, halved lengthwise (can substitute ¼–½ tsp red pepper flakes)

1 (13.5-oz (400-ml)) can unsweetened coconut milk

⅓ cup (86 g) smooth peanut butter

2 tbsp (30 ml) less-sodium soy sauce

2 tbsp (28 g) packed light brown sugar

1½ tbsp (23 ml) fresh lime juice

2 tsp (10 g) kosher salt, divided

Let's make the satay. Whisk the peanut oil, soy sauce, *shugá*, ginger, garlic and lime zest in a large bowl until combined. Toss the chicken tenders into the marinade to evenly coat. Cover and refrigerate to marinate, 30 minutes to 2 hours. Remove the chicken from the refrigerator and let it come to room temperature, leaving it in the marinade, for 30 minutes prior to grilling.

Now, make the peanut sauce: Add the oil to a 2-quart (1.9-L) saucepan over medium-low heat. Add the garlic, ginger and chiles or red pepper flakes and sauté until you smell the *gálick* and ginger, about 45 seconds. Add the coconut milk, peanut butter, soy sauce, brown *shugá*, lime juice, ½ teaspoon salt and ⅛ teaspoon pepper. Whisk until well blended. Bring to a gentle bubble over medium-high heat. Reduce the heat and let the sauce simmer and cook until the flavors build and the sauce slightly thickens, 10 to 15 minutes, whisking periodically. Remove the pan from the heat. Keep the peanut sauce warm until you're ready to serve. This sauce will yield about 1¾ cups (420 ml), a good indicator to know if you have reduced it enough.

Crank the grill or grill pan over medium heat. Spear and thread two tenders on each (6-inch (15-cm)) wooden skewer, creating a zigzag shape, making 16 to 20 skewers. Don't scrunch the chicken too tight onto the skewer or it won't cook evenly. Season the chicken with the remaining salt and pepper on both sides.

(Continued)

CHICKEN SATAY *with* PEANUT SAUCE *(continued)*

½ +⅛ tsp fresh finely ground black pepper, divided

3–4 tbsp (3–4 g) chopped cilantro

When the grill is well heated, oil the grill grates with a wad of heavy-duty paper towels, using tongs. Be careful! The paper towels should not be dripping with oil, rather just coated. Be sure to brush quickly. Grill the chicken until just cooked through and tender, 2 to 3 minutes on each side, 4 to 6 minutes total time. Careful not to torch the wooden skewers, position the handles towards the unlit side of the grill. You could soak them ahead, but I've found it's not always effective. Grill in batches, if using a grill pan. Remove the skewers from the grill and let them rest, 5 minutes, loosely tented with foil.

Serve the chicken skewers on a large platter with warm peanut sauce in a ramekin on the side for dipping. Garnish the chicken with cilantro, because you're fancy.

Chefie Tip:
Use a teaspoon to peel the ginger, it's easier!

GRILLED CHICKEN ENCHILADAS ROJAS

I love the slightly smokey, charred flavor in this dish, plus you can cook the chicken in only 8 minutes! Oh yeah! It's hands down the easiest and BEST chicken *EVAH!* Use this as your base to build great dishes, no need for any spices. It's so juicy, delicious and perfect for these enchiladas. If you're wondering why I prefer organic, in my opinion, it's juicier and tastes better. That's why it can stand alone with just salt and pepper.

Makes 4 to 6 servings

FOR THE ENCHILADAS

2 dried ancho chiles

2 dried guajillo chiles

1½ lbs (681 g) boneless, skinless chicken breasts (organic preferred)

¼ cup (60 ml) avocado oil + more for oiling the chicken

3 tsp (16 g) kosher salt, divided + more for seasoning the roux

1 tsp freshly ground black pepper, divided + more for seasoning the roux

1 small onion, diced

2–3 green onions, sliced, whites and dark greens separated

1 small Serrano chile, stemmed, seeded and minced

5 large cloves garlic, minced

¼ cup (31 g) all-purpose flour

2 tbsp (30 ml) chipotle adobo sauce (just the sauce)

2 tsp (4 g) ground cumin

2 tsp (4 g) ground coriander

3 cups (720 ml) chicken stock, preferably homemade (page 51)

Rinse the dried chiles very well (they can be sandy). Then fully submerge them in bubbling hot water to soak off the heat. Let them sit until soft and tender, about 30 minutes. Drain, removing the stems and seeds. You can prep these up to one day ahead.

Preheat the oven to 375°F (190°C) and heat your grill or grill pan over medium heat. Place the chicken in a large zip-top bag, push out all the air and zip closed. Pound the chicken breasts to an even thickness, using the flat side of a meat mallet. This will help them to cook evenly. Remove the breasts from the bag, drizzle a little oil over the chicken and season with 1½ teaspoons (8 g) of salt and ½ teaspoon of pepper on both sides. When the grill is well heated, oil the grill grates with a wad of heavy-duty paper towels, using tongs. Be careful! The paper towels should not be dripping with oil, rather just coated. Be sure to brush quickly. Grill the chicken until golden and just cooked through, 4 to 5 minutes on each side. Don't overcook it! Remove the chicken from the grill and set on a cutting board to rest, 8 minutes. Dice the chicken.

Place a 12-inch (30-cm) sauté pan over medium heat and add the ¼ cup (60 ml) of oil. When the oil is heated, add the onion, whites of the green onions and Serrano chile. Season with salt and pepper and sauté until tender, 2 to 3 minutes. Add the garlic, and sauté until you smell the *gálick*, about 30 seconds. Slowly whisk in the flour, a little at a time, until smooth. Cook the roux to build a nutty flavor, about 1 minute.

(Continued)

GRILLED CHICKEN ENCHILADAS ROJAS
(continued)

FOR THE PICO DE GALLO

3 ripe tomatoes, diced

1 small Serrano chile, stemmed, seeded and minced

⅓ cup (4 g) packed chopped cilantro + extra

2 limes, divided (zest and juice of one lime for the pico and one wedged for garnish)

1 tsp kosher salt

¼ tsp freshly ground black pepper

12 (5½-inch (14-cm)) corn tortillas

2 cups (224 g) freshly shredded Pepper Jack or Monterey Jack cheese

Add the drained, rehydrated chiles, chipotle sauce, cumin and coriander and slowly pour in the chicken stock while whisking, until fully blended. Season with 1½ teaspoons (8 g) of salt and ½ teaspoon of pepper and bring to a full bubble over medium-high heat, then reduce to medium-low. Continue cooking until all the flavors are combined and the sauce is velvety, about 10 minutes, whisking periodically. Don't let the sauce stick! Season to taste. Add the sauce to a blender and purée until smooth, holding the lid with a towel, so the heat doesn't blow off the top.

Meanwhile, make the pico de gallo. Toss the tomatoes, Serrano chile, cilantro, lime zest, lime juice, salt and pepper in a large bowl until combined.

To assemble the enchiladas, spray a 9 x 12–inch (23 x 30–cm) baking dish with non-stick cooking spray. Spread half of the chile sauce over the bottom of the pan, to coat. Divide the chicken and pico de gallo (using a slotted spoon) among 12 tortillas, spreading it down the middle lengthwise. You will have a little pico left over, so save that to garnish (makes it pretty!). Keep remaining tortilla shells covered while you work.

Roll up each tortilla and place each seam side down into the prepared baking dish, snuggling next to each other (lining two tortillas horizontally side by side across the pan lengthwise), to fit evenly. Pour the remaining chile sauce down the center of the tortillas, exposing 1 inch (2.5 cm) of the ends. It'll seem saucy but donta you worry! Sprinkle the cheese evenly over the sauce. Bake until hot and bubbly, 22 to 25 minutes. Remove the pan from the oven and let the enchiladas rest to set, for 10 minutes. As they sit, they'll further absorb the chile sauce.

Garnish with the leftover pico de gallo, green onions and cilantro. Serve lime wedges on the side, for squeezing.

INDOOR BARBECUED PULLED PORK
with HONEY COLESLAW

This easy, satisfying comfort food is not just for game day; it's perfect for a fall evening by the fire or hanging by the pool on a summer day and easily feeds a small crowd! You can also use this barbecue spice rub for ribs or chicken. Keep it in a tightly covered container and use it as you need it. It's best to prepare the coleslaw up to several hours ahead and marinate in the refrigerator for best *flavah!* The longer it sets, the better it gets!

Makes 8 to 10 servings

FOR THE HONEY COLESLAW

1 cup (240 ml) mayonnaise, preferably homemade (page 41)

¼ cup (60 ml) rice vinegar

3 tbsp (45 g) sugar

1 tbsp (15 ml) honey

6 cups (420 g) thinly sliced Savoy or green cabbage (½ medium head)

1½ cups (165 g) shredded carrots

1½ tsp (7 g) kosher salt

½ tsp fresh finely ground black pepper

FOR THE PULLED PORK

1 (4½–5½ lb [2–2.5 kg]) bone-in pork shoulder (also called pork butt)

1 tbsp (6 g) ground cumin

1 tbsp (8 g) granulated garlic powder

1 tbsp (7 g) smoked paprika

½ tsp cayenne pepper

3 tsp (15 g) kosher salt

1 tsp fresh finely ground black pepper

Avocado oil

1 cup (240 ml) barbecue sauce

8–10 fresh Kaiser rolls, split

To make the coleslaw, whisk the mayo, vinegar, *shugá* and honey in a large bowl. Toss in the cabbage and carrots, season with the salt and pepper and stir until well combined. Cover and refrigerate to marinate for several hours. To make the coleslaw with a pop of color, substitute some of the Savoy or green cabbage for a little red cabbage. Makes it pretty. Remove the coleslaw from the refrigerator 20 minutes before serving and give it a toss.

To make the pulled pork, remove and trim most of the excess fat from the pork; there will be some within the meat that you can't get to, but donta you worry, it'll melt while cooking, flavoring the pork and keeping it moist.

Stir the cumin, garlic powder, paprika, cayenne pepper, salt and pepper in a small bowl. Place the pork into a 9 x 12–inch (23 x 30–cm) baking dish. Lightly drizzle a little oil all over the pork and slather the spice rub all over the meat to evenly coat. If the spices are still dry, drizzle a tad more oil to hydrate them. We don't want them to burn. Let the pork sit at room temperature, to remove the chill and allow the spice rub to penetrate the meat, 30 minutes.

Preheat the oven to 350°F (175°C) and adjust the oven rack to the middle position.

(Continued)

INDOOR BARBECUED PULLED PORK *with* HONEY COLESLAW *(continued)*

Slather the barbecue sauce over the top of the pork and pour 2 cups (480 ml) of cold water into the bottom of the baking dish. Cover the baking dish with foil, sealing the edges to prevent the moisture from escaping; you may need to use two pieces of foil, overlapping to ensure a firm seal. Roast until tender, juicy and easily shredding when pulled with two forks, 3½ to 4 hours. The liquid should have reduced by about half or a little less when it's finished cooking.

Remove the pork from the oven and check to make sure it's easily shredding with two forks. If it needs more time, tightly cover it again and return to the oven; if it's uber tender, then let it rest, uncovered, about 20 minutes. Shred the pork with two forks into the barbecue juices and toss to coat all the meat with the sauce, discarding the bone.

Divide the shredded pork among the bottoms of 8 to 10 of the Kaiser rolls, top the pork with desired amount of coleslaw and finish with the roll tops. Serve immediately—no one wants soggy buns.

PECAN-CRUSTED PORK TENDERLOIN with ROSEMARY BROWN BUTTER

Traditionally, a standard breading procedure includes flouring first, but I've found over the years it's not necessary because oftentimes, the flour adheres to the coating and then pulls away from the meat after cooking. Only using eggs and coating creates a direct contact to the meat. It works like a charm when I use breadcrumbs. But because nuts are a little heavier than breadcrumbs, some may fleck off when preparing this, but donta you worry! Coating ahead of time and using a sharp knife while slowly slicing will help keep it pretty. If some nuts fall off, don't fret, it's still insanely delicious!

Makes 3 to 4 servings

1¼ cups (150 g) pecan halves

1¼ lbs (568 g) pork tenderloin, any excess fat trimmed

1¼ tsp (6 g) kosher salt + more for seasoning the rosemary butter

½ tsp fresh finely ground black pepper

2 large eggs

2 tbsp (30 ml) avocado oil

½ cup (1 stick [112 g]) unsalted butter, cut into pats

3 large fresh rosemary sprigs, needles removed + extra sprigs for garnish

Preheat the oven to 400°F (200°C).

In a food processor fitted with the steel blade attachment, pulse to chop the pecans until finely ground. Add the ground nuts to a wide shallow bowl.

Cut the pork tenderloin in half crosswise (making two individual logs to fit inside the pan side by side). Season the pork with the salt and pepper.

Whisk the eggs in another wide shallow bowl. Dredge the pork into the eggs, dripping off the excess. Then coat the pork with the pecans, pressing the ground nuts all the way around to adhere to the meat—you'll use all the pecans. Set the pork aside for 30 minutes at room temperature to moisten the pecans, preventing the crust from cracking. You can prepare the encrusted pork up to several hours ahead and refrigerate, then remove from the refrigerator and bring to room temperature, 30 minutes prior to cooking.

(Continued)

PECAN-CRUSTED PORK TENDERLOIN
with ROSEMARY BROWN BUTTER (continued)

Place a 10-inch (25-cm) oven-safe frying pan over medium heat for 1 minute. Add the oil. When the oil is heated and shimmers, add the pecan-crusted pork and sear until golden, 1 minute on three sides, a total of 3 minutes. Reduce the heat to medium-low, if the nuts are browning too quickly. Put the pan in the oven and roast the pork until cooked to medium doneness (internal temperature about 145°F (65°C)), 10 to 14 minutes, flipping the pork halfway through the cook time. Remove the pork from the oven and place on a cutting board to rest, 8 minutes. Being very careful and using an oven mitt, as the pan will be very hot, drain off the oil from the pan.

Return the pan to the stove over medium heat, add the butter and rosemary and slowly but constantly swirl the pan until the butter melts and is golden, 2 to 3 minutes. Season with a pinch of salt. Remove the pan from the heat.

Slice the pork into 1-inch (2.5-cm) rounds and arrange on a serving platter. Drizzle the rosemary brown *buttah* over the top. Garnish with extra rosemary sprigs around the pork, because you're fancy.

SESAME SALMON *with* SWEET JALAPEÑO UDON NOODLES

This dish is packed with big, bold, fresh and delicious Asian *flavah!* You could eat the salmon and noodles separately, but eating them together makes this a rockstar dish! Because the Serrano chile is being puréed in the blender, naturally cranking up the heat, add a little of it at a time and taste to make sure you reach your desired spiciness. Udon are Japanese wheat-flour noodles; if you can't find them, you can substitute soba noodles.

Makes 4 servings

FOR THE SAUCE

1 large clove garlic, roughly chopped

3 tbsp (45 ml) freshly squeezed lime juice

¾ cup (180 ml) mirin

½ cup (120 ml) less-sodium soy sauce

¼ cup (24 g) roughly chopped, peeled ginger

1 Serrano chile, stemmed and seeded as desired, roughly chopped

½ tsp kosher salt

½ cup (8 g) packed cilantro leaves

FOR THE SALMON

1 tsp kosher salt

½ tsp ground ginger

½ tsp granulated garlic powder

½ tsp fresh finely ground black pepper

1 (1½-lb (681-g)) center-cut salmon fillet, skin removed and cut crosswise into 4 pieces

5 tsp (15 g) sesame seeds

2 tbsp (30 ml) avocado oil

1 (9.5-oz (270-g)) package udon or soba noodles

Cilantro leaves, for serving

1 large lime, cut into wedges, for serving

Let's make the sauce: Add the garlic and lime juice to a blender and blend on medium to low speed until puréed. The lime juice mellows the *gálick*. Add the mirin, soy, ginger, desired amount of the Serrano chile and salt and purée until smooth. Add the cilantro and blend on low speed until finely chopped, 5 to 10 seconds, leaving small flecks of leaves in the sauce. Pour half of the sauce into a large mixing bowl and pour the remainder into a medium serving bowl.

Bring water to a rolling bubble in a 6-quart (5.7-L) pot over high heat.

Meanwhile, get the salmon going: Add the salt, ginger, granulated garlic and pepper to a small bowl and stir. Rub the spice blend over the salmon on both sides.

Spread the sesame seeds on a plate and press the top (the presentation "pretty" side) of each salmon filet into the sesame seeds to evenly coat the surface.

(Continued)

SESAME SALMON *with* SWEET JALAPEÑO UDON NOODLES *(continued)*

Add the oil to a 12-inch (30-cm) non-stick frying pan over medium to medium-low heat for 1 minute. Add the salmon, sesame seed side down, and sear until lightly golden, about 2 minutes, being careful not to burn the seeds! Flip and increase the heat to medium. Sear until golden and cooked to medium doneness, 1½ to 2 minutes. Don't overcook the salmon or it won't be tender and moist! Remove the salmon from the pan and place on a plate to rest, 5 minutes.

Add the noodles to the bubbling water and cook until tender, about 4 minutes. Check the package directions of the noodles you're using, however—I've found several brands cook faster than the package directs, so taste a noodle as you go. Drain and immediately toss the noodles into the large mixing bowl with the sauce, while they're still hot, so they absorb the sauce.

Divide the udon noodles among four shallow bowls and top with the fish. Spoon some of the extra sauce over the fish and garnish with extra cilantro leaves. Serve lime wedges on the side for squeezing. Eat with chopsticks, it makes a difference.

Chefie Tip:
Ask the fishmonger to remove the skin; it's easier!

VEAL MILANESE

It's the simple things that taste the best. I'll guide you through using the right heat at the beginning to ensure a crispy exterior and perfectly cooked interior. Veal cutlets are thin and cook fast, so it's crucial. And pan size always matters when cooking. If a certain pan is called for in a recipe, trust the process. A 10-inch (25-cm) pan is preferred for better control when cooking here.

From making Milanese with both chicken and veal my entire life, I've found there's no need for the flour before the egg wash; I know it's standard breading procedure, but it pulls away from the meat when frying and when you cut it, the breading separates. Eliminating the flour ensures the breading sticks directly to the meat.

Makes 2 servings

2 large eggs

¾ cup (82 g) Italian-style breadcrumbs

¾ lb (340 g) thinly sliced veal cutlets (about 4 cutlets)

1 tsp kosher salt + more for sprinkling

½ tsp freshly ground black pepper

½ cup (120 ml) safflower or peanut oil

1 lemon, cut into 4 wedges

Whisk the eggs in a large, shallow bowl. Place the breadcrumbs in a separate large, shallow bowl.

Carefully pound the veal with the textured side of a meat mallet on both sides; if you have a meat tenderizer with needle blades, better yet—it makes the veal nice and tender. Season the veal with salt and pepper on both sides and dredge it into the egg wash, dripping off the excess, then dredge and coat with the breadcrumbs, shaking off the excess. Set aside on a plate.

Place a 10-inch (25-cm) frying pan over medium-high heat until the pan is hot, about 1 minute. Add the oil. When the oil is heated and shimmers, about 1 minute, add the veal, working in two batches. Pan-fry until golden brown around the edges, 1 to 1½ minutes. Flip. Pan-fry until golden on the other side, about 1 minute.

If you're using a 12-inch (30-cm) frying pan, reduce the temperature to medium heat and you'll still need to cook in two batches, because all four cutlets may not fit comfortably in the pan. We want the meat to be crispy and not to steam.

Remove the veal to a wire rack placed on a large rimmed sheet pan. Lightly sprinkle with salt. Repeat with the remaining veal. Let the meat rest for 5 minutes.

Serve with lemon wedges on the side for squeezing over the veal.

RESTAURANT-STYLE CRAB CAKES *with* SRIRACHA RÉMOULADE

I learned how to make crab cakes while interning at the Fountain Restaurant at the Four Seasons Hotel in Philadelphia many years ago. They made the best! They were plumped nicely with good lump crabmeat and not too bready. That drives me nuts when restaurants do that! No one wants a crab cake loaded with breadcrumbs! You'll be proud to serve these and happy to eat 'em. They're so good!

Makes 4 servings

FOR THE CRAB CAKES

5 tbsp (75 ml) avocado oil, divided

1 cup (160 g) small-dice red bell pepper

1 cup (160 g) finely diced onion

1 tsp kosher salt, divided

Fresh finely ground black pepper

1 large egg

¼ cup (60 ml) mayonnaise, preferably homemade (page 41)

1 tbsp (15 ml) Dijon mustard

¼ cup (13 g) chopped dill

1 tsp sriracha

⅓ cup (36 g) seasoned Italian breadcrumbs

1 lb (454 g) lump crabmeat, drained and shells removed

3 tbsp (42 g) unsalted butter, at room temperature

Place a 12-inch (30-cm) oven-safe frying pan over medium heat. Add 2 tablespoons (30 ml) of the oil and heat the pan until the oil shimmers. Toss in the bell pepper and onion and season with ½ teaspoon of salt and a pinch of pepper. Sauté until tender, 5 to 6 minutes. Remove the pan from the heat and set it aside to cool.

Grab a large bowl and whisk the egg, mayo, mustard, dill, sriracha, ½ teaspoon of salt and a pinch of pepper until combined. Add the breadcrumbs and the cooled bell pepper and onion, also scraping out the oil from the pan, using a rubber spatula and adding to the bowl. Break apart the crab and add it to the bowl. Mix well until combined with clean hands, don't be a wimp! If the mixture is too loose and not forming a cake, add a tad more breadcrumbs, but not too much—the egg will help it to set in the oven.

Using a 3-inch (8-cm) ring mold, fill and pack the crab mixture, forming four cakes. You can also use a 3-inch (8-cm) ramekin or 1-cup (240-ml) measuring cup, but if you use either, spritz with non-stick cooking spray first, so the mixture doesn't stick when removing. Set the molded cakes on a baking sheet or clean plate. Cover and refrigerate the crab cakes to let them set, for at least 20 minutes and up to a few hours.

(Continued)

RESTAURANT-STYLE CRAB CAKES *with* SRIRACHA RÉMOULADE *(continued)*

FOR THE SRIRACHA RÉMOULADE

Zest of ½ lemon

1 tbsp (15 ml) freshly squeezed lemon juice

1 small clove garlic

1 cup (240 ml) mayonnaise, preferably homemade (page 41)

3 sweet gherkins, minced (¼ cup (60 g))

1 tbsp (15 g) drained, rinsed capers, chopped

1 tsp sriracha

1 tsp apple cider vinegar

¼ tsp kosher salt

Pinch fresh finely ground black pepper

Preheat the oven to 375°F (190°C).

Place the reserved pan over medium heat. Add the remaining 3 tablespoons (45 ml) of oil and heat the pan until the oil shimmers. Add the crab cakes and sear until golden brown, about 2 minutes. Reduce the heat to medium-low if they're browning too quickly. Carefully flip the crab cakes, immediately place the skillet into the oven and bake until warmed through and set, 15 to 17 minutes.

Meanwhile, to make the rémoulade, add the lemon zest and juice to a medium bowl, finely grate the garlic into the lemon juice and stir to mellow the *gálick*. Add the mayo, gherkins, capers, sriracha, apple cider vinegar, salt and pepper and mix well until combined. Cover and refrigerate until ready to serve.

When the crab cakes are finished baking (see Chefie Tip), remove the pan from the oven and return the pan to the stove over medium heat. Be careful, don't forget the pan is HOT, use your oven mitt when handling the pan! Add the butter to the pan and let it melt. Tilt the pan so the butter pools on one side and, using a tablespoon, scoop up the butter and baste the tops of the crab cakes until the butter foams in the pan, about 30 seconds to 1 minute.

Remove and divide the crab cakes among four plates. Serve with sriracha rémoulade on the side for dipping.

Chefie Tip:

To test if the crab cakes are done, insert a paring knife into the center of the crab cake for a few seconds when they come out of the oven. Then carefully place the flat side of the knife onto the back of your wrist: When it's hot, they're done.

HOMEMADE MARINARA with PASTA FROM SCRATCH

Don't you dare use store-bought sauce, you're better than that! This is so simple and *BETTAH!* If you grow plum tomatoes in your garden, even better: Use ripe ones after removing the skin. When I first started cooking as a young girl it was my mission to make a good yet simple marinara and delicious meat-a-ballz (as my Nana called them). I thought, I'm an Italian American girl who loves to cook, so mine has to be good. I worked on it for many years, and when I realized less is more, I found the right homemade, fresh flavor and have been making it this way ever since. If you're wondering why I drain the San Marzanos, it's just my preference. I like the flavor better without the purée, but if I'm making a ragù or bolognese, sometimes I leave it because the excess liquid is needed for a long braise time.

Makes 4¹/₂ to 5 cups (1.1 to 1.2 L)

1 lb (454 g) pasta, preferably homemade (page 86)

¼ cup (60 ml) olive oil

1 large onion, diced (about 1 cup [160 g])

2½ tsp (15 g) kosher salt, divided

1 tsp fresh finely ground black pepper, divided

5 cloves garlic, minced

½ cup (120 ml) chardonnay

2 (28-oz [794-g]) cans whole peeled San Marzano tomatoes

1½ tsp (2 g) dried parsley

1½ tsp (1 g) dried basil

1 tbsp (14 g) unsalted butter

Parmigiano-Reggiano or Pecorino Romano wedge

Fresh basil, sliced

If you're making the pasta homemade, you'll want to make the dough now, and while it's resting, we'll come back to the sauce.

Add the oil to a 4-quart (3.8-L) heavy-bottomed pot over medium heat. Add the onion, season with ½ teaspoon of salt and ¼ teaspoon of pepper and sauté until tender, 2 to 3 minutes. Add the *gálick* and sauté until you can smell it, about 30 seconds.

Deglaze with the wine and reduce the liquid by half, 1 to 2 minutes. Drain the San Marzano tomatoes and place the tomatoes into a medium bowl, then crush them with clean hands. Don't be a wimp! Add the tomatoes to the pot and fill the cans one-quarter of the way with cold water, gently swirling the cans to release the tomato juices from the walls of the cans, then add the liquid from both cans to the pot.

Add the parsley and basil, season with 2 teaspoons (10 g) of salt and ¾ teaspoon of pepper and stir until combined. Bring to a gentle bubble over medium-high heat. Reduce the heat to medium-low and cook until the flavors build, 25 to 30 minutes, stirring often. Don't let the sauce stick!

(Continued)

HOMEMADE MARINARA *with* PASTA FROM SCRATCH *(continued)*

If you're making the pasta, once the dough has rested, now's a good time to roll it out.

For a smoother texture to the marinara, pulse blend a few times in a food processor or use a handheld emulsion blender. If you blend it too fast or too long, the color will become more of a blush, less of a red; or leave it as is for a more rustic sauce.

Remove the sauce from the heat and stir in the butter until melted. Season to taste. Toss the cooked pasta into the marinara for a few minutes to absorb some of the sauce. Grate cheese over top and garnish with fresh basil when you're ready to serve. Serve family style.

Chefie Tip:
You can refrigerate the marinara in a tightly sealed container up to 3 days or freeze for up to 2 months.

PASTA *from* SCRATCH

When you get the hang of making pasta, you can make homemade pasta and marinara together in about 1 hour 20 minutes. Not bad for preparing both homemade. You can also make this recipe using only all-purpose flour; if you do, use 11 ounces (312 grams) total. You can also do this by hand with a rolling pin.

Makes a tad more than 1 lb (454 g). 6 to 8 servings

5½ oz (156 g) "00" Italian pasta flour + extra

5½ oz (156 g) durum wheat semolina

½ tsp kosher salt + more for cooking

3 large eggs

Olive oil

Place the flour, semolina and salt into a food processor, fitted with the steel blade attachment and pulse a few times to blend. Add the eggs and while the food processor is running, drizzle in ice-cold water in a slow steady stream, 1 tablespoon (15 ml) of water at a time, through the feed tube until the flour mixture lumps into a ball; this happens quickly. Two tablespoons (30 ml) is usually enough. As soon as the mixture crumbles together into a ball, immediately stop adding the water and turn off the food processor. Transfer the dough ball onto a lightly floured work surface and knead the dough to form into a round disk. Rub a touch of olive oil over the dough and tightly wrap with plastic wrap. Allow it to rest for 30 minutes at room temperature or overnight in the refrigerator. At this point, you can make tubular-shaped pasta, following the directions of a KitchenAid pasta press attachment.

Using a bench scraper, divide the dough into six equal portions. Work with one at a time and keep the remaining portions tightly covered while you work. Lightly dust flour onto your work surface. Flatten the piece of dough, then feed it through a KitchenAid pasta attachment at the widest setting (#1), with the stand mixer on medium speed (#6). Fold the dough like a letter into thirds, then feed it through the pasta attachment again. Repeat this step three to four times on setting #1, until the dough is smooth. This process is like kneading the dough. If the dough is feeling damp or sticky at any point in the process, lightly dust with flour so it doesn't stick to the roller. Repeat the flour dusting as needed.

(Continued)

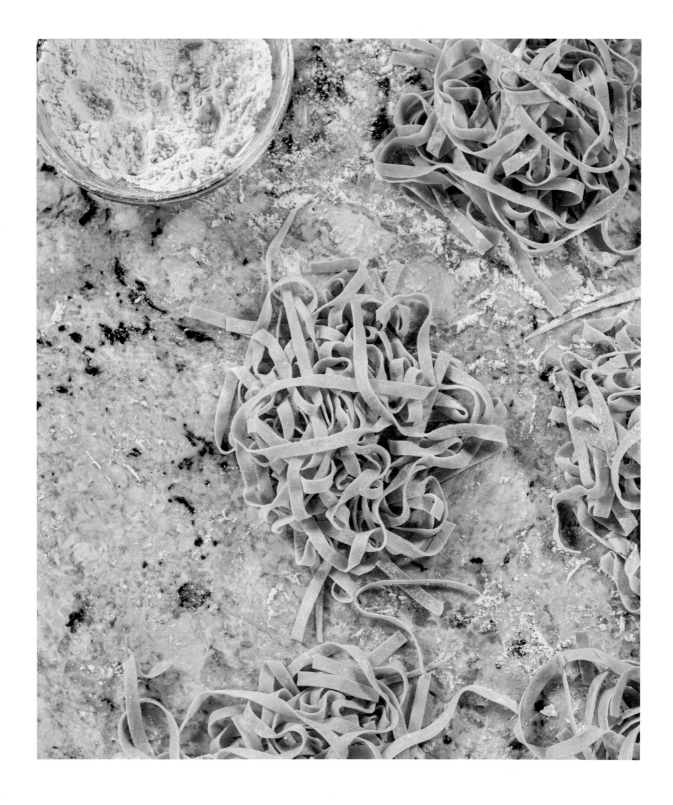

PASTA from SCRATCH (continued)

Increase the dial to setting #2, then fold the dough in half (not thirds) and feed it through, repeating this step one to two times. Continue feeding the dough through one to two times on each setting until you reach setting #6. When you reach setting #6, only pass it through one time and don't fold. You could keep going to setting #8, but I've found the dough rips.

Lay the pasta sheet onto a lightly floured piece of wax or parchment paper and cover with a clean kitchen towel while you repeat the process with the remaining dough. Do not stack the pasta sheets or they'll stick together. At this point, you can make lasagna, ravioli or tortellini, just to name a few.

When all the pasta sheets are rolled out, change the attachment to the desired fettuccine or spaghetti cutter. Feed the pasta sheets straight through, one at a time, on medium speed (#6) and place onto a lightly floured wax- or parchment paper–lined, rimmed baking sheet. Sprinkle the noodles with a little extra flour and gently toss each bundle, shaking off the excess flour, lightly coating the noodles, so they don't stick together. Cover the pasta nest with a clean kitchen towel. It's not necessary to dry out the noodles, they will break too easily. If you are preparing the pasta ahead, leave the kitchen towel over the pasta on the sheet pan, cover the whole thing with plastic wrap and refrigerate up to 1 day or flash freeze, then gently remove the pasta nests to freezer zip top storage bags and freeze up to 1 month. Don't stack anything on top of the bags or the pasta will break. When you're ready to cook frozen pasta, don't thaw it- just boil it an extra minute or two.

To cook the pasta, bring generously salted water to a rolling bubble in a 6-quart (5.7-L) pot while the pasta is resting. Plunge the pasta into the water and stir gently so it doesn't stick. Cook until the pasta tightens and forms the noodles, 2 to 3 minutes. Drain the pasta, reserving 1 cup (240 ml) of pasta liquid, in case you need it to thin the sauce. Return the pasta to the pot, pour the marinara over top and stir over low heat for a few minutes to marry the two, letting the sauce absorb into the pasta.

Chefie Tip:
Here is your cheat sheet for rolling out the pasta:

SPEED IS ON #6 THE ENTIRE TIME

#1 - 3–4 times, folding like a letter
#2 - 1–2 times, folding in half
#3 - 1–2 times, folding in half
#4 - 1–2 times, folding in half
#5 - 1–2 times, folding in half
#6 - 1 time, do not fold

CINNAMON PENNE *with* BUTTERNUT SQUASH AND KALE

Crisp air, the smell of wood burning in fireplaces, hayrides while apple picking; these are all the things I love about the fall season, and this dish is totally reminiscent of that. You can serve it as a vegetarian main dish or as a side dish to grilled chicken, roasted chicken or pork.

Makes 6 To 8 servings (for a main dish)

1 (2–2¼ lb (908 g–1 kg)) butternut squash, peeled, seeded and ¾-inch (2-cm) dice

2 tbsp (30 ml) avocado oil

1½ tsp (7 g) kosher salt, divided

½ tsp fresh finely ground black pepper, divided

1½ tsp (4 g) ground cinnamon, divided + extra to garnish

¾ cup (90 g) chopped pecans

¾ lb (340 g) penne rigate (for homemade, see Chefie Tip)

½ cup (120 ml) good-quality olive oil, divided

5 cloves garlic, sliced

1 large shallot, sliced

1 large bunch kale (6–8 cups (110–150 g) torn packed leaves), stems discarded

Preheat the oven to 400°F (200°C). Group the squash chunks in the middle of a rimmed baking sheet, drizzle avocado oil over the squash, season with ¾ teaspoon of salt, ¼ teaspoon of pepper and ½ teaspoon of cinnamon and toss to coat. Spread the squash out evenly and roast until tender and slightly caramelized, about 25 minutes. Scatter the pecans over the squash and return to the oven to warm them through, 2 minutes. Remove the pan from the oven and season the squash with more salt and pepper to taste.

Meanwhile, get the pasta going: Bring a 6-quart (5.7-L) pot of salted water to a rolling bubble over high heat. Toss in the penne and stir. Cook until tender, 12 to 15 minutes. It'll taste better tender than al dente, so the pasta can absorb the *gálick* oil.

Place a 12-inch (30-cm) sauté pan over medium heat. Add 2 tablespoons (30 ml) of olive oil. When the oil is heated and shimmers, add the garlic and shallot and season with a pinch of salt and pepper. Sauté until you can smell the *gálick*, about 45 seconds. Add the remaining 6 tablespoons (90 ml) of olive oil to the pan and reduce to simmer, to infuse the oil with the *gálick*, 1 minute. Add the kale, increase the heat to medium and season with ¾ teaspoon of salt and ¼ teaspoon of pepper. Toss the kale to coat with the oil, until wilted but still vibrant green, about 2 minutes. Remove the pan from the heat.

Drain the penne and return it to the pot. Add the garlic-oiled kale, butternut squash, pecans and remaining 1 teaspoon of cinnamon to the pot with the penne and toss well to combine. Season to taste. Divided among plates or pasta bowls and serve hot. Lightly sprinkle with extra *cinny-mon* on top, because you're fancy!

EAT *Your* VEGGIES!

When you start with beautiful, blemish-free, fresh vegetables and cook and season them right, it's the most amazing thing in the world! Every Friday night, Andreas and I eat at the same steakhouse with our good friends Skip and Jeannette; we've been doing this for more than 15 years, and I often only order vegetable side dishes as my meal. They're that good—but they're even better when you make them at home!

I'll show you how to make sauces and glazes, and we'll create caramelization from a high-temperature oven, charring from the grill or a skillet to turn bland, simple veggies into tender and super-flavorful side dishes that you can totally eat as a meal.

In this chapter, we'll cook a variety of vegetable dishes for every season, even for the holidays, but honestly, you can eat them all year round. Jewel Candy Sweet Potatoes (page 103) is my family's recipe, I've been eating these since I was a kid. They use only four ingredients and you just toss them into one pot for the most delicious, candy-sweet and savory side dish that everyone goes crazy for! If you wanna make greens that are a bit heartier, try my Sautéed Swiss Chard with Cannellini Beans (page 117), and my Cypriot Cinnamon Potatoes with Dill Yogurt (page 108) are so darn good. *Cinny-mon* on potatoes? YASSS! Try those, too! I guess at some point, you'll realize I'm obsessed with vegetables!

ROASTED CAULIFLOWER with PIGNOLI

Pignoli means pine nuts. It's Italian! Caramelized cauliflower rocks—roasting imparts a depth of flavor you just can't resist. This dish is meaty, savory, slightly salty from the Parmigiano-Reggiano and bright from the lemon zest, then finished with a nutty, crunchy pop from the pignoli to complete it. It's sure to be your new go-to side dish for any night of the week.

Makes 4 to 6 servings

1 large head (2½–3 lbs (1.1–1.4 kg)) cauliflower, washed, dried well and cut into florets (see Chefie Tips)

⅓ cup (80 ml) good-quality olive oil

1½ tsp (7 g) kosher salt

½ tsp fresh finely ground black pepper

2 tbsp (15 g) pine nuts

Zest of 1 lemon (see Chefie Tips)

1–2 tbsp (6–12 g) freshly grated Parmigiano-Reggiano

2 tbsp (8 g) chopped Italian parsley

Preheat the oven to 425°F (220°C).

Group the florets into the center of a large rimmed baking sheet, drizzle the oil over top and toss well to evenly coat. Gather the florets back into the center, season with salt and pepper (but don't toss or the seasoning will fleck off) and spread them apart, so they cook evenly. Roast until tender and golden, 25 to 28 minutes, tossing halfway through the roasting time.

Sprinkle the pine nuts over the cauliflower and return to the oven until they're lightly toasted and warmed through, 1 to 2 minutes.

Remove the cauliflower from the oven and place it on a small serving platter. Zest the *limón* over the top of the cauliflower and sprinkle with Parmigiano-Reggiano. Garnish with parsley and serve family style. Because you're fancy!

Chefie Tips:
When prepping the florets, cut halfway through the stem, using a paring knife, then pull them apart. This keeps the flower pretty!

Wrap the zested lemon tightly with plastic wrap and refrigerate, so it doesn't dry out.

GRILLED SUMMER VEGETABLES *with* DILL YOGURT

This dill yogurt is the sauce that keeps on givin'. I also use it for my Cypriot Cinnamon Potatoes (page 108), and it's equally delicious on salmon or chicken, too. It's a good, easy go-to when you want to whip up a sauce in a hurry. When you're grilling this summer, pair these veggies with grilled pork, steak, chicken or fish and if you have any left over, use 'em for my Briám with Baked Eggs (page 123) the next morning, which is simple yet insanely delicious.

Makes 8 to 10 servings

FOR THE DILL YOGURT SAUCE

Grated zest of ½ a lemon

2 tbsp (30 ml) freshly squeezed lemon juice

1 small clove garlic

1 tsp honey

1⅔ cups (250 g) 2% or 5% plain Greek yogurt

⅓ cup (15 g) chopped dill

½ tsp kosher salt

¼ tsp cayenne

FOR THE SUMMER VEGETABLES

3 tbsp (45 ml) freshly squeezed lemon juice

¼ cup (60 ml) good-quality olive oil

1 tbsp (15 g) sugar

2½ tsp (12 g) kosher salt, divided

Fresh finely ground black pepper

To make the sauce, add the lemon zest and juice to a medium bowl. Grate the garlic into the bowl and stir. It mellows the *gálick*. Stir in the honey until blended, add the yogurt, dill, salt and cayenne and stir until evenly combined. Set aside.

Heat the grill to medium to medium-low (adjusting the temperature as you grill to prevent burning). It's best to do this on a grill rather than a grill pan, because you'll need a lot of surface area to grill all of the vegetables.

For the vegetables, add the lemon juice to a medium bowl. Add the olive oil, *shugá*, ½ teaspoon of salt and a crack from the pepper mill and whisk until the *shugá* is dissolved.

Season all the vegetables on both sides with 2 teaspoons (10 g) of salt and 15 cracks of the pepper mill. Brush half of the lemon vinaigrette all over the vegetables, on both sides.

(Continued)

GRILLED SUMMER VEGETABLES *with* DILL YOGURT *(continued)*

1 bunch green onions

2 large red bell peppers, quartered lengthwise, stemmed and seeded

1 large red onion, sliced into ½-inch (1.3-cm)-thick rings

2–3 medium zucchini, halved lengthwise

2 small Italian eggplants, sliced crosswise ½ inch (1.3 cm) thick

1 bunch asparagus, ends trimmed

1 lemon, cut in half crosswise

Fleur de sel or sea salt

When the grill is well heated, oil the grill grates with a wad of heavy-duty paper towels, using tongs. Be careful! The paper towels should not be dripping with oil, rather just coated, and be sure to brush quickly. Place the vegetables onto the grill, working in two to three batches. Cover and grill until slightly charred and tender, flipping the vegetables over once. Grill the green onions for 2 to 3 minutes; the red peppers and red onion for 5 to 6 minutes; the zucchini, eggplant and asparagus for 8 to 12 minutes; and the halved lemon to just warmed through with slight char marks, 1 to 2 minutes. These grilling times are just a guide; it's best to grill the vegetables until tender yet slightly crisp with an even char, cradling your heat from medium to medium-low as needed. You can also remove them to the non-lit side of the grill to control the charring while grilling.

Place the vegetables on a large platter and brush them with the remaining lemon vinaigrette. Season to taste and lightly garnish with fleur de sel or sea salt for that pop of crunchy, salty texture. Arrange the charred *limón* halves around the vegetables, for squeezing. Serve the dill yogurt in a medium bowl on the side to dollop over the vegetables.

ROASTED CARROTS *with* GOAT CHEESE

This is a perfect side dish for the holidays, but you can certainly enjoy it any time. These tender, sweet roasted carrots have an earthy farm-to-table freshness with a creamy tang from the goat cheese and a pop of crunch from the pistachios and pomegranate arils. It's so easy to whip together any night of the week.

One day while cooking with master chef from France Olivier Desaintmartin, I noticed him scraping, not peeling, the whole carrots. The difference in flavor is unparalleled. If you peel the carrots, two things happen: You lose that fresh, rustic appearance, but more importantly you lose the intense, earthy flavor that makes these carrots sheer perfection! Don't peel the carrots!

Makes 4 servings

1½–1¾ lbs (681–795 g) carrots or rainbow carrots with their green tops

3 tbsp (45 ml) olive oil + more for serving

¾ tsp kosher salt + more for serving

¼ tsp fresh finely ground black pepper + more for serving

Preheat the oven to 425°F (220°C).

Trim the tops off the carrots, leaving 2 inches (5 cm) of the stems attached to the carrots, and leave the tips of the carrots—those stringy ends get deliciously crispy when roasted. Using a paring knife, position the knife blade at an angle and scrape the carrots, all the way around, removing a thin layer, cleaning the carrot. Do not peel! Wash the carrots under cold water and dry them completely. This will remove any dirt, leaving the delicious, sweet earthy flavor.

If the carrots are larger than ½ inch (1.3 cm) thick, slice them in half lengthwise, leaving the trimmed tops intact; otherwise, leave whole. Leaving the tops makes for a farm-fresh-to-table presentation. Because you're farm fresh fancy!

Place the carrots on a large rimmed baking sheet and toss with the oil. Season with the salt and pepper and roast until lightly caramelized and tender, 25 to 30 minutes.

(Continued)

ROASTED CARROTS *with* GOAT CHEESE
(continued)

Extra-virgin olive oil

2 oz (56 g) chèvre (goat cheese)

3 tbsp (25 g) pomegranate arils

3 tbsp (11 g) roasted salted pistachios, roughly chopped

Italian parsley leaves

Remove the carrots from the oven and place them on a medium serving platter, staggering and arranging all of the tops facing in one direction. Using a rubber spatula, transfer any accumulated roasting juices, oil and salt from the baking sheet and pour over the carrots—that's good *flavah!* Drizzle a little extra-virgin olive oil over the carrots. Season with more salt and freshly ground black pepper.

Break apart and scatter small dollops of the goat cheese, pomegranate arils and pistachios over the carrots. Garnish with parsley. Because you're extra fancy!

Chefie Tip:
If entertaining, you'll want to double this recipe for a larger party. Divide the carrots among two baking sheets and alternate on oven racks, rotating them halfway through the baking time for even caramelization.

JEWEL CANDY SWEET POTATOES

When I was growing up, my family called these yams, it's how the supermarkets labeled them; however, they're actually sweet potatoes, jewel sweet potatoes, to be exact. Here's my inspired version of the ones my mom made every Thanksgiving and Easter. They're the star side dish, perfectly paired with savory turkey and salty ham. Everyone looks forward to them twice a year—the tradition has been passed down and lives on. I hope it becomes your family's favorite, too!

Makes 6 to 8 servings

3 lbs (1.4 kg) fresh jewel sweet potatoes, peeled and cut into ½-inch (1.3-cm) rounds

1 lb (454 g) dark brown sugar

½ cup (1 stick (112 g)) unsalted butter, cut into 8 pieces

½ tsp kosher salt

In a 6-quart (5.7-L) heavy-bottomed pot or Dutch oven, add all the ingredients and pour 1 cup (240 ml) of water over the top. Bring to a rapid bubble over medium-high heat, then reduce the heat to medium-low and cover with the lid vented. It is very important to not put the lid on tightly, or the liquid can bubble over; don't walk away, regardless! Cook until the liquid reaches three-quarters of the way up the sides of the sweet potatoes, 8 to 10 minutes.

Remove the lid and gently rotate the sweet potatoes from the bottom to the top periodically to cook them evenly, but do this gently so you don't break them! Cradle the heat between medium and medium-low for a gentle bubble. Cook until fork tender, 15 to 18 minutes. Keep an eye on the pot so they don't boil over!

As the sweet potatoes become fork tender, remove each one with a slotted spoon to a heat-safe serving bowl until they're all tender. Cook the candied liquid over medium heat until it has thickened and coats the back of a spoon, 4 to 6 minutes. Drizzle the hot candied syrup from the pot over the sweet potatoes. Serve immediately.

Chefie Tip:
Peel and cut the sweet potatoes up to 1 day ahead and store in a large zip-top bag in the refrigerator.

STEAKHOUSE CREAMED SPINACH

I've been making this easy, one-pot side dish for a very long time, and when I posted it on my Pinterest and YouTube channel, it became incredibly popular! Pair it with prime rib, steak or chicken for the holidays or any night of the week.

Makes 4 to 6 servings

5 tbsp (70 g) unsalted butter

4 cloves garlic, minced

½ cup (80 g) sliced shallots

¼ cup (31 g) all-purpose flour

1¼ cups (300 ml) whole milk

Pinch of freshly grated nutmeg

1½ tsp (7 g) kosher salt + more for seasoning the spinach

½ tsp freshly ground black pepper + more for seasoning the spinach

1 lb (454 g) pre-washed fresh baby spinach

1 cup (85 g) freshly shredded good-quality Gruyère cheese

Melt the butter in a 6-quart (5.7-L) heavy-bottomed pot or Dutch oven over medium heat. Toss in the *gálick* and shallots and sauté until tender, about 1 minute.

Slowly whisk in the flour until smooth, about 1 minute. Slowly whisk in the milk until smooth and season with the nutmeg, 1½ teaspoons (7 g) salt and ½ teaspoon pepper. Bring the sauce to a gentle bubble over medium heat, then reduce to simmer and cook until the raw flour flavor cooks out, 3 to 5 minutes, whisking constantly to prevent burning. The mixture will be a loose paste, similar to the texture of loose mashed potatoes. Donta you worry!

Tear the spinach into smaller pieces and stuff all of it into the pot. Season with more salt and pepper. Cover and increase the heat to medium, to steam and slightly wilt the spinach, about 1 minute. Remove the lid and stir with a rubber spatula and tongs, rotating the spinach from the bottom over the top of the fresh spinach, further wilting all of the spinach. Keep tossing and stirring until all the spinach has wilted, releasing its liquid, thinning the sauce, about 2 minutes. Remove from the heat. Season to taste with more salt and pepper.

Stir in the Gruyère until melted. Spoon the spinach into a small casserole dish and serve family style.

MEXICAN STREET CORN (Esquites)

Esquites, also known as *elote en vaso*, means toasted corn. Mexican food is my #1 favorite cuisine to eat and to cook because the flavors are bright, bold and fresh. I love creating my take on classics like this street fare food, traditionally eaten in a disposable cup with a plastic spoon. Buy queso fresco or cotija in its whole form and crumble it yourself—it's creamier!

Makes 5 To 6 servings

2 tbsp (30 ml) freshly squeezed lime juice

2 tsp (10 g) sugar

⅔ cup (80 g) crumbled queso fresco or cotija, divided

½ cup (120 ml) mayonnaise, preferably homemade (page 41)

½ cup (120 ml) sour cream

⅓ cup (5 g) roughly chopped cilantro + extra

1 chipotle in adobo, finely minced + 1 tsp adobo sauce

1 tsp chili powder

1 tsp paprika

1¾ tsp (8 g) kosher salt, divided + more for sprinkling on the corn

½ tsp fresh finely ground black pepper, divided

6 ears of corn, husked

Avocado oil

Preheat the grill, set to medium, for 10 minutes.

Meanwhile, let's make the sauce: Whisk the lime juice and *shugá* in a large bowl until the *shugá* dissolves. Add ⅓ cup (40 g) of queso fresco or cotija, and the mayo, sour cream, cilantro, chipotle and adobo sauce, chili powder, paprika, ¾ teaspoon of salt and ¼ teaspoon of pepper into the bowl and whisk until smooth.

Lightly brush the corn cobs with oil to thinly coat and sprinkle with salt. Place the corn on the grill and lower the lid. Grill until lightly charred all over, turning one-quarter turn every 2 minutes. Total grilling time will be about 8 minutes. If the corn is getting too charred, lower the heat to medium-low or low and continue grilling with the lid down. If you hear the corn pop, donta you worry! It does that.

Remove the corn and set aside until cool enough to handle, about 5 minutes. Cut the corn off the cob (see Chefie Tip) and add it to the bowl with the mayonnaise mixture. Season with 1 teaspoon of salt and ¼ teaspoon of pepper and stir until fully combined. Scoop into a serving bowl or individual cups, served with a spoon.

Garnish with the remaining queso fresco or cotija and a couple tablespoons (2 g) roughly chopped *ci-läntrrō* (roll the r, be authentic!).

Chefie Tip:
So you don't make a mess, grab a large bowl and place a smaller bowl inside the large bowl, upside down. Place a damp, folded paper towel on top of the small bowl and place the flat side of the corn cob onto the paper towel. Cut and remove the corn kernels from the cob.

CYPRIOT CINNAMON POTATOES *with* DILL YOGURT

My husband's family is Cypriot and they use a lot of kanéla (cinnamon). It's Greek! Cinnamon pairs great with meats, potatoes and desserts, both sweet and savory. It's heavenly! I rarely make anything traditional; I like to take inspiration from everywhere and add a twist for my own take. That's how I roll! My family never complains.

Makes 6 servings

4–5 Idaho russet potatoes

½ cup (120 ml) olive oil

2 tbsp (4 g) roughly chopped fresh thyme leaves

1 tsp ground cinnamon

2½ tsp (12 g) kosher salt

½ tsp fresh finely ground black pepper

Dill Yogurt (page 97)

Dill sprigs

Preheat the oven to 425°F (220°C). Position the oven racks so one rack is near the top of the oven and one is near the bottom of the oven. Peel, rinse and dry the potatoes well with heavy-duty paper towels. Slice the potatoes in half lengthwise, then cut them lengthwise into 1-inch (2.5-cm)-thick, long, fat, rustic potato wedges.

Toss the potatoes in a large bowl with the oil, thyme, cinnamon, salt and pepper until evenly coated. Grab two rimmed baking sheets and divide the potatoes among them, drizzling any remaining oil from the bowl over the potatoes. Do not use one sheet pan! If the potatoes are too crowded, they will steam and not get slightly crispy. Place one sheet on the upper rack and the other on the lower rack and bake until golden on the bottom, about 20 minutes.

Remove the potatoes from the oven and flip a spatula upside down to chisel under the potatoes from the sheet pans, to release, but don't break them! Flip the potatoes over and place them back into the oven, rotating the bottom sheet pan to the top rack and vice versa. Continue baking until tender and lightly golden, another 8 to 14 minutes. Don't brown them too much or they'll lose the flavor of the *cinny-mon*.

Remove the potatoes from the oven and serve with the dill yogurt on the side for dipping. Garnish with dill sprigs, because you're fancy!

ROASTED BEETS *and* GOAT CHEESE SALAD *with* LEMON VINAIGRETTE

Sweet roasted, earthy beets are the star here. They're surrounded by crisp, crunchy celery, peppery radishes, fresh dill and creamy goat cheese, then finished with a very simple lemon vinaigrette. Pair this salad with fish, scallops or chicken for a light lunch or dinner. If purchasing beets with their green tops, save the greens to braise, sauté or you can even toss them into your smoothie, raw. Don't forget the French baguette for sopping up the beet *limón* vinaigrette. So good! This is what fresh, simple food is all about.

Makes 3 to 4 servings

3 red beets (7–8 oz [198–227 g] each)

Avocado oil

¼ tsp kosher salt + more for sprinkling

Fresh finely ground black pepper

Zest and juice from 1 large lemon

3 tbsp (45 ml) good-quality extra-virgin olive oil

1½ tsp (8 g) sugar

3–4 large radishes, trimmed, halved and sliced (about ¾ cup (85 g))

3 large celery ribs, sliced on an angle

¼ cup (13 g) chopped fresh dill

½ cup (8 g) celery leaves

2 oz (56 g) chèvre (goat cheese)

1 fresh French baguette

Preheat the oven to 400°F (200°C). Line a rimmed baking sheet with foil, making sure it reaches all the way to the ends of the sheet.

Clean the beets with cold water and dry them well. Place the beets on the foil-lined baking sheet. Rub the beets with a little avocado oil all over and lightly sprinkle with salt and pepper. Fold the sheet of foil in half, over the top of the beets, sealing and crimping the edges to tightly close, creating a pouch, so no steam escapes. Roast until tender, about 1 hour 10 minutes. If your beets are smaller in size (4 to 5 ounces (113 to 142 g) each), they'll need less time, 45 minutes to 1 hour.

Meanwhile, make the lemon vinaigrette: Add the lemon zest and juice, extra-virgin olive oil, *shugá* and ¼ teaspoon of salt to a medium bowl and whisk vigorously until emulsified. Set aside.

Remove the beets and carefully open the hot, steamy foil pouch, to check for doneness. Insert a paring knife into the beets, it should go in very easily. If the beets need more time, seal the foil pouch back up, return to the oven and continue roasting until tender. When the beets are done roasting, rip open the foil pouch and set them aside to cool.

(Continued)

ROASTED BEETS and GOAT CHEESE SALAD with LEMON VINAIGRETTE (continued)

When the beets are cool enough to handle, trim and discard the ends. Place the beets inside a heavy-duty paper towel and rub off the skin, working one at a time. Halve the beets and cut each half into wedges. Add the beets to a medium bowl with two-thirds of the vinaigrette and toss to evenly coat. Season with more salt and pepper and arrange on a medium serving platter, along with the vinaigrette from the bowl.

In a separate medium bowl, toss the radishes, celery and dill with the remaining vinaigrette. Season with salt and pepper. You'll want to toss them separately so the beets don't stain the celery and radishes—this will keep it pretty.

Arrange the radish mixture over the beets, along with the vinaigrette from the bowl. Garnish with celery leaves and pull small crumbled pieces from the goat cheese log to dollop evenly over the salad. Serve with a fresh French baguette for sopping up the juices.

Chefie Tip:
The beets can stain, so wear an apron and wash your hands regularly as you work.

ASIAN-STYLE COCONUT BROCCOLI

This dish comes together quickly so you need to be on your A game, but I know you can do it because you're a rockstar! Prepping all your ingredients ahead—called mise en place, which means everything in its place—will set you up for success and keep you organized as you quickly stir-fry this side in 5 minutes. You can blanch and leave the broccoli on a clean kitchen towel up to several hours ahead at room temperature, until you're ready to stir-fry.

Makes 4 to 6 servings

2 lbs (908 g) fresh broccoli crowns, cut into florets (see Chefie Tips)

¾ tsp kosher salt, divided + more for cooking

6 tbsp (90 ml) avocado oil, divided

4 cloves garlic, minced, divided

1 tbsp (12 g) minced, peeled ginger root, divided (see Chefie Tips)

½ tsp red pepper flakes, divided

Fresh finely ground black pepper

¼ cup (60 ml) less-sodium soy sauce

2 tbsp (30 ml) mirin

3 tbsp (21 g) sweetened coconut flakes

Bring lightly salted cold water to a rolling bubble in a 6-quart (5.7-L) pot over high heat. Add the florets and par-cook until tender-crisp, 3 to 4 minutes. The water will not return to a bubble when you add them in, donta you worry! Time it as soon as you add them.

While the broccoli is cooking, add lightly salted cold water to a large bowl, filling halfway. Toss in several handfuls of ice and stir well. Drain the broccoli and immediately plunge it into the salted ice bath to stop the cooking and lock in the bright green color, but only for 1 to 2 minutes, we don't want to waterlog the broccoli. Remove the ice, drain and place the broccoli onto a clean kitchen towel. Pat dry.

Place a wok or 12-inch (30-cm) frying pan over medium-high heat for 1 minute. If using a non-stick frying pan, you may need less oil. Add 3 tablespoons (45 ml) of the oil, and when it is heated and shimmers add half the garlic, half the ginger, half the red pepper flakes and half the broccoli and season with half of the salt and a couple cracks from the pepper mill. Stir-fry until you can smell the *gálick* and ginger and the broccoli is warmed through, 1 to 1½ minutes, tossing constantly. If you feel the pan is dry, add a tad more oil.

Empty the broccoli into a large bowl, scraping out the garlic and ginger, so they don't burn. Repeat and stir-fry the second batch of the broccoli with the remaining oil, garlic, ginger, red pepper flakes, salt and a couple cracks from the pepper mill.

(Continued)

ASIAN-STYLE COCONUT BROCCOLI
(continued)

When the second batch of broccoli is cooked, add the first batch of the broccoli to the wok or pan. Pour in the soy sauce and mirin and stir-fry constantly until reduced by half, 1 to 1½ minutes.

Pile the broccoli onto a large serving platter, using a slotted spoon, leaving the sauce in the wok or pan to continue reducing until slightly bubbly, 10 to 30 seconds. Pour the sauce over the broccoli, adding all the garlic and ginger too. The broccoli should be tender-crisp like an Asian broccoli stir-fry. Sprinkle the coconut over top of the broccoli and serve family style.

Chefie Tips:
When prepping the florets, cut halfway through the stem, using a paring knife, and then pull apart. This keeps the flowers pretty.

Use a teaspoon to scrape and peel the ginger, it's easier.

SAUTÉED SWISS CHARD *with* CANNELLINI BEANS

You don't need a lot of chicken stock for this recipe, but I find when I keep 1 quart (1 L) of homemade chicken stock (page 51) on hand in the refrigerator, I can use it for sauces, vegetables, potatoes, rice and more all week long. Cooking dried cannellini beans in your pressure cooker is a time saver. No preservatives, and tastes better! Soak 1 cup (212 g) of beans for 4 to 6 hours and pressure cook in 8 cups (1.9 L) water with a touch of oil and some aromatics on HIGH for 10 minutes. Do a quick release, then strain. Season to taste with kosher salt. This will yield about 2 cups (364 g) of cooked beans. They're creamy and delicious! For other bean varieties, cook times vary. If using canned, 1 (15-ounce [425-g]) can equals 1¾ cups.

Makes 3 to 4 servings

1 large bunch chard (rainbow, red or green)

2 tbsp (30 ml) olive oil

¾ tsp kosher salt, divided + more for serving

¼ tsp fresh finely ground black pepper, divided + more for serving

4 cloves garlic, minced

1 large shallot, sliced

¼ tsp red pepper flakes

1¾ cups (318 g) cooked cannellini beans (if using canned, drained and rinsed)

¾ cup (180 ml) chicken stock, preferably homemade (page 51)

1 tbsp (14 g) unsalted butter

Fresh Italian bread

Remove the stems from the chard and tear the leaves. Wash the stems, cut them into ½-inch (1.3-cm) pieces and set aside. Triple wash the leaves and dry on a clean kitchen towel; you'll have about 8 to 9 cups (234 to 296 g) of leaves and about 2 cups (190 g) of stems.

Add the oil to a 12-inch (30-cm) sauté pan over medium-low heat. When the oil is heated, add the chard stems, season them with ¼ teaspoon of salt and ⅛ teaspoon of pepper and sauté until tender-crisp, 5 to 6 minutes, cradling the heat between medium and medium-low.

Add the garlic, shallot and red pepper flakes and sauté until the *gálick* is fragrant and the shallot is tender, about 1 minute. Add the beans and chicken stock and bring to a gentle bubble over medium heat. Pile in the chard leaves. The pan will be overflowing at this point, donta you worry! Just jam it all in, season with ½ teaspoon of salt and ⅛ teaspoon of pepper and cover the pan with a lid until the chard leaves are slightly wilted, about 1 minute.

Remove the lid and gently toss (being careful not to break the beans!) until the chard leaves are wilted, 1 to 2 minutes. Remove the pan from the heat and stir in the butter until melted. Season to taste, as desired. Serve on a small serving platter with fresh crusty Italian bread on the side.

CHAMPIONS EAT BREAKFAST!

I always eat breakfast, no matter what, even if I'm running late. It's fuel to jump-start my day, and because you're a champ, you need yours, too!

When I develop recipes it's not about me, it's about you! That's why I became a chef, to create from my knowledge, inspiration, passion and palate to bring joy to your lives and tummies! My family loves breakfast, so I created these dishes for them, and I hope you'll enjoy them, too.

We'll make simple, light breakfast eats to beautiful brunch dishes, but if you want to eat these for dinner, do it! Because you can! There are no rules in my kitchen. Homemade food is love and you should enjoy whatever, whenever you want!

We'll make the best Strawberries and Cream Protein Shake (page 133) *EVAH* (no electric mixer); tender Easy Homemade Blueberry Muffins (page 125); Cranberry-Almond Granola (page 130) your way; and a classic Greek vegetable casserole dish called Briám with Baked Eggs and Garlic Crostini (page 123) to glam up your Sunday brunch.

You got this champ!

BUTTERMILK BLUEBERRY FLAPJACKS

My popular Classic Homemade Pancake recipe has been seen over 9.8 million times on TikTok with more than 1.5 million likes. I have to say, these are even *bettah!* You don't even need butter or syrup. Eat 'em as is, if you want!

Makes 12 to 13 pancakes. 6 to 8 servings

2 cups (250 g) all-purpose flour

¼ cup (50 g) sugar

1½ tsp (7 g) baking soda

1 tsp kosher salt

1½ cups (222 g) fresh blueberries

2 cups (480 ml) low-fat buttermilk

¼ cup (56 g) unsalted butter, melted, cooled + more at room temperature for serving

2 large eggs

Avocado oil

Maple syrup

Whisk the flour, *shugá*, baking soda and salt in a large bowl. Rinse the berries in a strainer with cold water, gently shaking off the excess water. Toss them in the flour to evenly coat the berries.

Whisk the buttermilk, butter and eggs in a separate large bowl until combined. Pour into the flour mixture and stir with a rubber spatula, until evenly combined. Be gentle: Don't Break the Berries! Let the batter rest for 10 minutes, to relax the gluten.

Meanwhile, crank the heat on a griddle to 350°F (175°C) or medium heat. If using a 12-inch (30-cm) non-stick frying pan, heat for 1 minute before ready to cook, over medium-low heat. Drizzle a little oil onto the griddle or into the pan. Using a heavy-duty paper towel, wipe up the excess oil while coating a thin layer over the griddle or pan.

Ladle the batter with a 2-ounce (59-ml) ladle onto the hot griddle or pan, working in batches. When the perimeters of the flapjacks are set and bubbles start to burst the surface, about 2 minutes, flip. Sometimes the bubbles burst, but not always. If the flapjacks are beginning to brown too quickly, reduce the heat to medium-low and cradle the heat between medium and medium-low. Cook the other side until cooked through and fluffy, 1½ to 2 minutes.

Place the pancakes on an oven-safe platter and keep warm on the lowest temperature setting in your oven, as you finish the rest.

Serve butter on the side for spreading and maple syrup on the table for everyone to drizzle over top, as they like.

BRIÁM with BAKED EGGS and GARLIC CROSTINI

This is a breakfast twist on a classic, summer vegetable dish called briám. It's Greek! Adding eggs and Kasseri makes it more substantial—or leave them out if you're vegan. Kasseri is a Greek sheep and goat's milk cheese that can be found in the cheese section at some markets, specialty stores or online. If you're entertaining, you can make the vegetables up to 4 hours ahead, place in a baking dish, cover with plastic wrap and keep at room temperature. When you're ready to serve, reheat the vegetables until hot before adding the cheese and eggs, then finish baking.

Makes 4 to 6 servings

FOR THE BRIÁM

1 eggplant

3 tsp (15 g) kosher salt, divided + more for sprinkling the eggplant

7 ripe Roma tomatoes, cored, quartered lengthwise and halved

2 zucchinis, quartered lengthwise, ¾-inch (2-cm) dice

2 red bell peppers, 1-inch (2.5-cm) dice

1 large red onion, 1-inch (2.5 cm) dice

16 garlic cloves, smashed

¼ cup (15 g) roughly chopped fresh oregano

⅔ cup (160 ml) olive oil

Zest of 1 lemon

2 tbsp (30 ml) freshly squeezed lemon juice

1½ tsp (3 g) freshly ground black pepper

Preheat the oven to 400°F (200°C). Set one oven rack in the top third of the oven and one on the bottom.

Peel and slice the eggplant lengthwise into four equal portions. Lightly sprinkle with salt and let it rest on paper towels to pull out some moisture and bitterness, about 25 minutes. While the eggplant is resting, prep the remaining ingredients.

Divide the tomatoes, zucchinis, red peppers, red onion, garlic cloves and oregano among two 13 x 18–inch (33 x 46–cm) rimmed sheet pans. Wipe the eggplant dry, removing the salt and moisture and dice into 1-inch (2.5-cm) cubes. Toss them evenly among the other vegetables.

Whisk the oil, lemon zest and juice in a small bowl. Divide the lemon oil over the vegetables and toss well to evenly coat. Season all of the vegetables with 2 teaspoons (10 g) of the salt and 1 teaspoon of the pepper. Spread out all the vegetables to evenly cook.

(Continued).

BRIÁM *with* BAKED EGGS *and* GARLIC CROSTINI *(continued)*

3 oz (85 g) freshly grated Kasseri cheese

6–8 large eggs, at room temperature

Coarse sea salt

2 tbsp (8 g) chopped Italian parsley

FOR THE GARLIC CROSTINI

5 tbsp (70 g) unsalted butter

3 tbsp (45 ml) good-quality olive oil

1 day-old French baguette, cut into ½-inch (1.3-cm) slices on a bias

Kosher salt and fresh finely ground black pepper

1 large clove garlic, cut in half crosswise

Chefie Tip:
Buy garlic cloves already peeled for recipes like this, that require a lot. It's easier.

Place one baking sheet on the upper third rack and the other on the bottom rack. Bake until tender, 20 minutes. Remove and toss the vegetables, spreading the vegetables back out among the baking sheets. Return to the oven, alternating the placement on the oven racks. Continue baking until lightly golden and the moisture has reduced by two-thirds, 20 to 25 minutes. Season all the vegetables with the remaining 1 teaspoon of salt and ½ teaspoon of pepper as needed.

Transfer the roasted vegetables to a 9 x 13–inch (23 x 33–cm) baking dish. Sprinkle the cheese over the vegetables and make slight indentations (the size of a half dollar, using the back of a tablespoon), in six to eight spots, evenly spread out. Crack one egg at a time and slowly release into an indentation. Don't break the yolks! Repeat with the remaining eggs. If you're adding more than six eggs, the whites may run together, donta you worry! Bake until the egg whites are set and the yolks have a skin but are still runny, 8 to 12 minutes. Remove the pan from the oven (leaving the oven on) and let the vegetables rest for 5 to 8 minutes. Keep warm.

To make the crostini, warm the butter and oil in a 2-quart (1.9-L) saucepan over medium-low heat until the butter is melted, about 2 minutes, slowly swirling the pot occasionally. Arrange the bread slices on a rimmed baking sheet and brush both sides with the oil *buttah*. Lightly sprinkle with kosher salt and finely cracked black pepper on one side. Bake the bread slices until lightly golden and toasted, 6 to 8 minutes. Remove and rub the surface of each slice with the cut garlic clove.

Sprinkle a pinch of sea salt over each egg, for a salted crunch, and garnish the vegetables with parsley, because you're fancy! Using a spatula, scoop deep under each egg in the vegetable mixture—don't break the yolks! Divide the briám among four to six plates. Serve with garlic crostinis on the side.

EASY HOMEMADE BLUEBERRY MUFFINS

Don't use a pre-mix box—you're better than that! We're baking these babies from scratch. No need to break out your stand or hand mixer either! This batter conveniently whips up in a bowl and bakes for 18 to 20 minutes, any morning you want.

You can find sanding *shugá* at most arts & crafts stores, kitchenware stores and some supermarkets or use *shugá* in the raw, which you can find at most supermarkets, that works great, too.

Makes 10 muffins

2 cups (250 g) all-purpose flour

2 tsp (9 g) baking powder

1 tsp kosher salt

1¼ cups (185 g) fresh blueberries (see Chefie Tips)

1¼ cups (250 g) sugar

2 large eggs

½ cup (120 ml) low-fat buttermilk

½ cup (120 ml) canola or vegetable oil

1 tsp pure vanilla extract

5 tsp (25 g) white sanding sugar or sugar in the raw, divided

Preheat the oven to 375°F (190°C). Place 10 cupcake liners into a 12-cup muffin pan (see Chefie Tips).

Sift the flour and baking powder into a large bowl. Add the salt and whisk to combine. Rinse the blueberries under cold water and gently shake to dry. Toss them into the flour mixture and stir to evenly coat the berries with the flour. This will help prevent the berries from sinking to the bottom of the muffins when baking. Add the *shugá* to the same bowl and gently stir to combine.

Whisk the eggs in a medium bowl, pour in the buttermilk, oil and vanilla extract and whisk to combine. Pour the buttermilk mixture into the flour mixture and stir, using a rubber spatula, until evenly blended. Do this gently: Don't Break the Berries! The texture should be slightly thick and gooey. Let the batter rest, to relax the gluten, about 10 minutes.

Divide the batter among 10 cupcake liners, using a cookie scoop if you have one, it's easier. Make sure you get all the batter out of the bowl by using a rubber spatula so that you can fill each liner— we want fluffy muffin tops! Sprinkle ½ teaspoon of sanding *shugá* or *shugá* in the raw over the top of each muffin.

(Continued)

EASY HOMEMADE BLUEBERRY MUFFINS
(continued)

Bake until the center is puffed, very lightly golden and when you insert a toothpick into the center, it comes out clean, 18 to 20 minutes.

Remove the muffins from the oven and as soon as they are cool enough to handle remove them from the pan and set them on a wire rack to cool. It's best to get them out of the pan as soon as you can, so they don't continue cooking.

Chefie Tips:
Lightly oil a paper towel and rub the surface and around the top of the cups of the muffin pan, to prevent any sticking.

Use fresh, in-season blueberries for the best muffins, but if you're using frozen blueberries, rinse them under cold water in a strainer, until the water runs clear. Drip dry before adding to the flour mixture.

PRESSURE COOKER STEEL CUT OATS

Cooking oats in a pressure cooker makes them taste so good! Plus it's easier, faster and infuses great flavor under pressure. However, if you don't have a pressure cooker you can make them in a pot on the stove too, just follow the cooking instructions on the packaging up to the salt and finish the oats the same, as instructed in the directions below. The eggs give protein and a fluffy, creamy texture to the oats. It's my husband, Andreas', trick that I've stolen. It's genius.

Makes 3 To 4 servings

3½ cups (840 ml) whole milk

1½ cups (240 g) steel cut oats

2 tbsp (28 g) unsalted butter

½ tsp kosher salt

2 large eggs, at room temperature, beaten

⅓ cup (73 g) packed light brown sugar

¼ cup (60 ml) good-quality honey

Fresh berries and/or ripe, sliced peaches, for serving

Add the milk, steel cut oats, butter and salt to a 6- or 8-quart (5.7- or 7.6-L) pressure cooker insert pot and stir. Pressure cook on HIGH for 10 minutes. When it's done cooking, turn off the pressure cooker or clear the functions, so it doesn't default to the warming cycle.

Allow for a natural release for 5 minutes, then quick release the remaining pressure. Unlock the lid and immediately begin quickly stirring. It may seem like there's not enough milk, donta you worry!

Slowly stream in the beaten eggs, a little at a time, while quickly stirring until thickened, about 1 minute. Stir in the *shugá* and honey until combined. Let sit to further thicken and carryover cook the eggs, about 2 minutes. Stir. The texture should be creamy like porridge.

Divide among three to four bowls and top with desired berries and/or peaches.

CRANBERRY-ALMOND GRANOLA

If you love granola, make your own—because you can! Here's a way you can control the ingredients and add whatever nuts, dried fruits or grains you like. Just swap mine out for your favorites. It's so easy. Layer granola in your favorite glass, alternating fresh berries with flavored Greek yogurt or skyr (an Icelandic thick and creamy high-protein cream), or sprinkle over vanilla ice cream for a crunchy texture. My husband, Andreas, likes to pour cold milk over it in a bowl and eat it like cereal. He says it's delicious.

Makes About 7 cups (770 g)

4 cups (360 g) old fashioned oats

¾ cup (91 g) dried cranberries

¾ cup (185 g) dried apricots, small dice

½ cup (48 g) sliced almonds

½ cup (64 g) salted, dry roasted sunflower seeds

⅔ cup (160 ml) good-quality honey

½ cup (110 g) packed dark brown sugar

¼ tsp kosher salt

Chefie Tip:
Spray your measuring cup with non-stick cooking spray before measuring the honey, it'll make it easier to release the honey from the cup.

Preheat the oven to 300°F (150°C) and spray a large rimmed baking sheet with non-stick cooking spray.

Place the oats, cranberries, apricots, almonds and sunflower seeds in a large bowl and toss to evenly combine. Set aside.

Add the honey, brown *shugá* and salt to a 2-quart (1.9-L) saucepan and place over medium-low heat. Stir the honey mixture until the *shugá* melts and liquifies, 2 to 3 minutes. Remove the pan from the heat.

Spray a rubber spatula with non-stick cooking spray—this will help when mixing the sticky granola mixture. Pour the honey mixture over the granola and quickly toss to evenly coat, using the spritzed spatula. Spread the oat mixture evenly over the prepared baking sheet.

Bake until the oats are toasted and lightly golden brown, 23 to 26 minutes, tossing halfway through the bake time. Remove the baking sheet from the oven and toss again.

As it cools and begins to harden, use the back side of a spatula to chisel any oats from the bottom of the baking sheet. Toss the granola a few more times as the mixture fully cools, hardens and sets.

Place the cooled granola in an airtight container and store at room temperature or in the refrigerator for up to 1 week.

STRAWBERRIES and CREAM PROTEIN SHAKE

My kids are athletes; my son, Costas, is a wrestler, my daughter, Isabella, plays field hockey, and my husband, Andreas, and I weight train regularly, so we all drink protein shakes in our house. I came up with this one to turn that chalky protein taste into yummy, delicious strawberries and cream *flavah!* If you drink protein shakes after a workout, for breakfast or for a late afternoon pick-me-up, try this one! You're welcome.

The frozen strawberries make this thick, frothy and shake-like. If making with fresh strawberries, add 1 cup (150 g) of ice cubes in addition to make it cold. It'll be thinner but still delicious.

Makes 1 (16-oz [473-ml]) shake

8–9 whole frozen medium-sized strawberries

½ cup (123 g) low-fat strawberry yogurt

¼ cup (60 ml) sweetened vanilla almond milk

1 scoop (⅓ cup (26 g)) vanilla whey protein powder

½ tsp pure vanilla extract

Put the strawberries, yogurt, almond milk, protein powder and vanilla into the large cup of a vitamin nutrient extractor (bullet blender), tightly screw on the lid/blade and shake to blend the protein powder, or put into a blender with a tight-fitting lid.

Purée until smooth and serve in a tall glass with a smoothie straw, because you're a champ!

APPLE PIE BREAKFAST PUDDING

It's all about texture here. Warm, creamy, porridge-like cereal brings me back to when I was a kid. I loved farina! I love the creamy texture! So, I had to create a gourmet version based around *cinny-mon*-sweetened apples for comforting *flavah*. My family loves it, I know yours will, too.

Makes 3 to 4 servings

2 small Fuji, Gala or Honeycrisp apples, peeled, cored and diced (about 2 cups (250 g))

4–5 tbsp (50–65 g) sugar

½ tsp ground cinnamon + extra to garnish

2 tbsp (28 g) unsalted butter

¼ tsp kosher salt

3 cups (720 ml) whole or 2% milk

½ cup (88 g) farina wheat cereal

Add the apples in one layer to the bottom of a 4-quart (3.8-L), heavy-bottomed pot. Depending on what kind of apples you're using, add 4 tablespoons (50 g) of *shugá* for sweeter apples and 5 tablespoons (65 g) for ones that need an extra boost of sweetness. Add the cinnamon, butter, salt and ½ cup (120 ml) water to the apples and stir. Bring to a bubble over high heat, stirring periodically. Reduce the heat to medium and cook the apples until the liquid is reduced by half and the cinnamon simple syrup coats the tender, yet still a bit crisp, apples, 6 to 9 minutes.

Pour the milk over the apples and bring to a gentle bubble over medium-high heat. Slowly whisk in the farina and return to a bubble. Reduce and cradle the heat between medium and medium-low and cook over a gentle bubble until thickened, 2 to 4 minutes, whisking periodically. Don't let the mixture stick to the bottom of the pot!

Remove the pot from the heat and let the mixture sit for 3 minutes to fully thicken. Your consistency should be thick and creamy like pudding. Divide among three to four bowls and garnish with *cinny-mon* lightly sprinkled on top—because you're fancy! Serve immediately.

EVERYTHING *SHUGÁ*

If you're wondering why I say *shugá*, it's because that's how my Theía Anthoula says it, in her cute Greek accent. One day her voice was in my head and it slipped out while filming my cooking videos and that was it!

Cooking is something that comes naturally to me, but baking I need to work at a bit harder. However, donta you worry! I will never share a dessert recipe or any recipe that isn't perfectly mastered! I'll obsess, research and test until it's right or I'll scrap it, to never be seen again. In 2010, I worked on the set of *Cake Boss* at Carlo's Bakery in Hoboken, New Jersey, traveling more than 4 hours to and from to learn from the best. I wanted to improve my skills to bring you more delicious desserts! I achieved the art of fondant cake layering and decorating and learned so many valuable tips to *per-fact* my dessert creations, making them even better.

Remember how I told you the freezer is your friend? That goes for baked goods, too! Have a birthday a week away and no time to bake fresh, delicious Red Velvet Cupcakes (page 160) or Carrot Cake with Cream Cheese Frosting (page 138) the day of? Bake the cupcakes or cake rounds up to one week ahead, let them cool completely, wrap the rounds in plastic wrap and place them in the freezer. Situate the cupcakes on a sheet pan, slide them into the freezer to flash freeze and when frozen, transfer the cupcakes to large zip-top bags. When you're ready to ice and decorate for celebrating, remove them to thaw at room temperature, it doesn't take long, 30 minutes to an hour, tops. They'll taste as fresh as if you just made them that day! I do this for all of my bread, too, even sandwich bread! Fresh every time!

Have you tried my Best Banana Bread (page 150)? It's famous! She got more than 25 million views and more than 4.3 million likes! I'm so proud of her! My countless attempts to make this bread perfectly moist and sweet was well worth the work.

Grab your aprons; let's bake! *Shugá* makes everyone happy!

CARROT CAKE *with* CREAM CHEESE FROSTING

My good friend Chantal's mom is an amazing baker; she makes the best carrot cake! Out of respect I could never ask for the recipe, so I had to create my version inspired by hers. It turned out so well and I've been making it ever since.

Makes 12 servings

FOR THE CARROT CAKE

1 cup (240 ml) canola or vegetable oil + more for the pans

2½ cups (313 g) all-purpose flour

1½ tsp (7 g) baking soda

1 tsp ground cinnamon

¼ tsp ground nutmeg

¼ tsp ground cloves

1 tsp kosher salt

1½ cups (300 g) sugar

3 large eggs, room temperature

2 cups (220 g) peeled, shredded carrots

½ cup (98 g) fresh minced ripe pineapple (can substitute canned, drained and minced)

½ cup (60 g) chopped pecans + extra to garnish

Preheat the oven to 375°F (190°C). Lightly grease two (8-inch (20-cm)) baking pans with oil, using a paper towel, then line the bottom of each pan with a parchment disk. If you're using larger or smaller baking pans, you'll need to decrease or increase the bake time to accommodate.

Sift the flour, baking soda, cinnamon, nutmeg and cloves into a large bowl. Add the salt and whisk to combine. Set aside. Mix the *shugá* and 1 cup (240 ml) oil on medium speed in a stand mixer fitted with the paddle attachment. Add the eggs one at a time, and mix until blended. Add the carrots, pineapple and pecans and continue blending on medium-high speed until combined, scraping down the sides of the bowl as needed.

Pour the flour mixture onto the center of a piece of parchment or wax paper, in a straight line about 18 inches (46 cm) long lengthwise. Carefully pick up the paper and slowly funnel in the flour, a little bit at a time, on low speed. This way, the flour won't waft all over you and make a mess. Gradually increase the speed to medium, scraping down the sides and under the bottom of the bowl's dimple, as needed until blended. Don't overmix! Divide the batter evenly between the prepared pans. Bake until the tops and centers are set and a toothpick comes out clean, 30 to 35 minutes. Remove the cakes from the oven and let them rest on a cooling rack for several minutes. Run a butter knife around the perimeter of each cake to loosen, and carefully remove the cakes, while they're still warm, so they will release more easily. Remove the parchment disks, place the cakes back onto the cooling rack and let them cool completely.

(Continued)

CARROT CAKE *with* CREAM CHEESE FROSTING *(continued)*

FOR THE CREAM CHEESE FROSTING

1 lb (454 g) cream cheese, softened

1 cup (224 g) unsalted butter, softened

4 cups (480 g) confectioners' sugar

1 tsp pure vanilla extract

To make the frosting, in a stand mixer fitted with the whisk attachment, cream the cream cheese and butter until smooth. Add the confectioners' *shugá* a little bit at a time (or funnel it in as you did for the cake) so you don't make a mess, and blend until smooth. Scrape down the sides as needed to evenly mix. Add the vanilla and mix. Cover and chill to firm up a bit.

When you are ready to frost the cake, place one cake round on a flat plate or cake stand and frost the top. Place the second cake round on top, hump side up, and frost the top and the sides, all the way around. Garnish with pecans on top.

Chefie Tip:

For baking success, when using cup measurements, spoon the flour into the measuring cup (never pack) and with a flat surface, like a butter knife, swipe the excess across the top. This also applies to the *shugá*. The best way to measure is to use a food scale.

BEACH BLUEBERRY PIE

Wanna make a delicious blueberry pie? This is it baby! This pie is inspired from one of my favorite restaurants, Steve and Cookie's By the Bay in Margate, New Jersey. They make the most amazing blueberry pie. After years of tasting and several attempts to get the blueberries to set just right, I found cornstarch along with pectin was the trick. Here's my copycat version of this yummy pie. Be patient and only make it when blueberries are in season, at their best. Dollop with homemade whipped cream, or I love it best with Häagen-Dazs vanilla ice cream—you deserve it!

Makes 8 servings

FOR THE GRAHAM CRACKER CRUST

1¼ cups (130 g) graham cracker crumbs

½ tsp ground cinnamon

2 tbsp (30 g) sugar

2 tbsp (28 g) packed dark brown sugar

8 tbsp (112 g) unsalted butter, melted

FOR THE FILLING

4 pints (38 oz [1 kg]) fresh blueberries, rinsed, divided

½ cup (100 g) sugar

½ cup (110 g) packed light brown sugar

3 tbsp (24 g) cornstarch or arrowroot

4 tsp (13 g) low-sugar fruit pectin (I use Sure Jell, pink box)

¾ tsp ground cinnamon

2 tbsp (30 ml) freshly squeezed lemon juice

Premium vanilla ice cream

Preheat the oven to 375°F (190°C).

Mix the graham cracker crumbs, *cinny-mon* and both *shugás* in a large bowl until evenly combined. Pour in the butter and evenly moisten, using the back of a fork. Transfer the mixture to a 9-inch (23-cm) pie plate. Shimmy the plate to even out the mixture. Use the bottom of a ramekin or drinking glass to press the mixture onto the bottom and gently press high up onto the sides of the pie plate, using the side of the ramekin or glass, to form the crust. Bake until lightly golden, 8 to 9 minutes. Remove the crust from the oven. The crust may puff up and the sides may shrink, donta you worry! Immediately but carefully press to flatten and form the crust, using the ramekin, but do this gently—don't crack it! Let the crust cool while you make the filling.

Now we make the filling: Purée 2½ cups (342 g) of blueberries in a food processor fitted with the steel blade attachment until smooth. Add the *shugás*, cornstarch or arrowroot, pectin, cinnamon and puréed blueberry mixture to a 2½-quart (2.4-L) saucepan and heat on medium-high, whisking until smooth. Bring to a rapid bubble, while constantly whisking, until the *shugás* have melted and the mixture has thickened, 2 to 4 minutes. You want to make sure the bubbles break the entire surface to ensure it fully thickens, and watch it carefully so it does not burn. Remove the pan from the heat and let the mixture cool at room temperature, about 20 minutes, stirring periodically to help the mixture cool faster.

(Continued)

BEACH BLUEBERRY PIE *(continued)*

Gently toss the remaining blueberries in a large bowl with the lemon juice, stirring gently so they don't break. Carefully fold the cooled, puréed blueberry mixture with the whole blueberries until the whole berries are evenly coated. Again, stir gently so you don't break the whole berries. Transfer the blueberry filling into the graham cracker shell with a rubber spatula, and evenly mound to form a slight dome in the center, while gently but firmly packing the filling all around.

Place the pie in the refrigerator to chill and set, at least 5 hours but overnight is preferred for best results to fully chill and slightly soften the crust for the perfect, crispy texture. When it is fully chilled, cover with plastic wrap. If serving after 5 hours, the crust may need a sharp chef's knife to remove the first piece, but donta you worry! Even if it doesn't look perfect, it's still friggen' delicious!

Cut into eight wedges and serve chilled with a scoop of vanilla ice cream on the side.

Chefie Tip:
Run your knife or pie cutter under warm water, then wipe dry to cut for clean slices. Repeat for each cut.

SALTED CARAMEL PECAN PUMPKIN CHEESECAKE

Here's a velvety and creamy cheesecake just in time for the fall season! No need for a bain-marie, which often cracked my cheesecakes anyway. After researching this technique, I found that a low-temperature oven was the trick for a foolproof, crack-free cheesecake! This is a make-ahead dessert. There's almost 2 hours baking time, 2 hours resting time and 3 hours plus refrigeration time; it's not hard to make and totally worth every minute of the wait. Plan ahead!

Makes 10 servings

FOR THE ROASTED PUMPKIN

1 (4-lb [1.8-kg]) sugar pumpkin or pie pumpkin

Avocado oil

FOR THE CRUST

1½ cups (156 g) graham cracker crumbs

2 tbsp (30 g) granulated sugar

¾ tsp ground cinnamon

4 tbsp (56 g) unsalted butter, melted

Preheat the oven to 400°F (200°C). Line a baking sheet with parchment paper.

Remove the stem from the pumpkin and cut it in half lengthwise, scraping out the insides, discarding the seeds or keeping them to roast later, if desired.

Rub a little oil over the pumpkin flesh and place the halves, flesh side down on the parchment-lined baking sheet. Roast the pumpkin until fork-tender, 35 to 45 minutes. Remove the pumpkin from the oven and let it cool. Pull away and discard the skin, mashing the pumpkin with a fork. Place the pumpkin in a food processor fitted with the steel blade attachment and purée until smooth. Set aside 1 cup (240 g) and store the rest in an airtight container and refrigerate 1 to 2 weeks for another use. If the purée seems watery, place it in a medium bowl, lined with cheesecloth. Pull the cheesecloth up and over the purée to twist and wring out any excess moisture. This will help give you baking success.

To make the crust, preheat the oven to 325°F (165°C).

In a large bowl, mix the graham cracker crumbs, *shugá*, *cinny-mon* and *buttah* until well combined. Lightly spray a 9-inch (23-cm) non-stick springform pan with non-stick cooking spray and add the graham cracker mixture, pressing evenly and firmly onto the bottom and ½ inch (1.3 cm) up the sides, using a ramekin or drinking glass. Bake until the crust is lightly golden, 8 to 10 minutes. Remove the pan from the oven and let the crust cool.

(Continued)

SALTED CARAMEL PECAN PUMPKIN CHEESECAKE *(continued)*

FOR THE CHEESECAKE

3 (8-oz (227-g)) packages cream cheese, softened, room temperature

1¼ cups (250 g) sugar

½ cup (120 ml) sour cream

1½ tsp (4 g) ground cinnamon

¾ tsp ground ginger

¾ tsp allspice

½ tsp freshly grated nutmeg

½ tsp ground cloves

4 large eggs, room temperature

2 cups (240 g) chopped pecans, toasted

1 cup (240 ml) caramel syrup

Coarse sea salt

Chefie Tip:
To toast the pecans, toss them in a skillet over low heat, for a few minutes until warmed through.

Decrease the oven temperature to 225°F (110°C) and open the door to help drop the internal temperature for a few minutes. Check the temperature read with an oven thermometer; once 225°F (110°C) is reached, close the door. This is a very important step, to ensure the oven is at the proper temperature, so the cheesecake doesn't crack!

In a stand mixer fitted with the whisk attachment, mix the cream cheese, 1 cup (245 g) pumpkin purée, *shugá*, sour cream, cinnamon, ginger, allspice, nutmeg and cloves until smooth. Add the eggs, one at a time, and beat until blended, scraping down the sides and under the dimple of the bowl until very smooth. Pour the cream cheese mixture into the cooled graham cracker crust and bake until set with a slight wiggle in the center, 1 hour 45 minutes. Turn off the oven and open the door to vent, leaving the cheesecake inside the oven for 15 minutes. This step prepares the cheesecake for room temperature, so it doesn't crack!

Place the cheesecake on a cooling rack to fully cool at room temperature, about 2 hours. Cover the springform pan with a clean kitchen towel, but be sure it is not touching the cake. Tightly tuck the towel under the pan and refrigerate until completely set, 6 hours to overnight. The towel is ideal to collect any condensation that forms from the cake. Adding plastic wrap will only drip the water droplets onto the cake, making it soggy.

When ready to serve, top the cake with the chopped toasted pecans (see Chefie Tip), remove the springform pan sides and slice into ten wedges. Place the caramel in a microwave-safe bowl and microwave on high until pliable and slightly warm but not hot, 10 to 15 seconds.

Drizzle some caramel over the pecans and lightly sprinkle with sea salt before serving. Makes it prettier this way: because you're fancy!

SUMMER PEACH COBBLER

Cobbler is a fruit-filled, classic American dessert, surrounded by a lumpy golden crust which resembles a cobbled road, which is how it received its name. When peaches are in season, that's the time to make this dessert. I've found when the peaches are perfectly ripe, they'll easily peel after blanching. When purchased from the farmers' market or grocery store, leaving them at room temperature for about 2 days gets them perfectly ripe. Planning ahead is key!

Makes 8 servings

3 lbs (1.4 kg) peaches (about 8–9 peaches), ripe but not mushy

1½ cups (300 g) sugar, divided

2 tbsp (30 ml) brandy

½ tsp kosher salt + extra

Preheat the oven to 375°F (190°C). Add cold water to a large bowl, filling halfway. Toss in a few handfuls of ice. Set aside.

Bring cold water to a rolling bubble in a 6-quart (5.7-L) pot over high heat. Cut a shallow X on the bottom of each peach, using a paring knife. Submerge the peaches in the bubbling water to blister the skin at the X, 30 seconds to 1 minute. Remove the peaches immediately when you see the skin peeling, using a slotted spoon, and place them in the ice bath, to stop the cooking. Let them sit in the cold water for a couple of minutes.

Peel and remove the skin, with a paring knife, starting at the scored X. If you find they are not easily peeling, use a vegetable peeler. Cut each peach in half, discarding the pit, and slice the peaches into ½-inch (1.3-cm) wedges.

Add the peaches, ½ cup (100 g) *shugá*, brandy and a pinch of salt to a 12-inch (30-cm) sauté pan. Bring to a bubble over medium-high heat and stir. Reduce the heat to medium-low and cook the peaches until softened yet still holding their shape, 10 to 11 minutes, stirring periodically so they don't burn. They'll release a good amount of liquid, donta you worry! Remove the pan from the heat.

(Continued)

SUMMER PEACH COBBLER *(continued)*

½ cup (112 g) unsalted butter

1½ cups (188 g) all-purpose flour

1½ tsp (7 g) baking powder

¾ cup (180 ml) whole milk, room temperature

2 large eggs, room temperature

Premium vanilla ice cream

Meanwhile, melt the butter and pour it into the bottom of a 9 x 12–inch (23 x 30–cm) baking dish, to evenly coat. In a large bowl, whisk the flour, remaining 1 cup (200 g) *shugá*, baking powder and the ½ teaspoon salt until combined. Pour in the milk, add the eggs and whisk until smooth. Let the batter rest for 10 minutes to relax the gluten. Pour the batter into the buttered baking dish to evenly coat the bottom. Do Not Stir! Using a slotted spoon, evenly spoon the peaches over the batter. Drizzle the remaining peach syrup over the peaches. Again: Do Not Stir!

Bake until the crust is lightly golden brown and cooked through, 38 to 42 minutes. Remove the cobbler from the oven and let it rest and set, about 30 minutes. The flavor is best after it sets, rather than ripping into it out of the gate.

Serve warm, cut into squares with a scoop of ice cream, served à la mode—because you're fancy!

Chefie Tip:

For baking success, when using cup measurements, spoon the flour into the measuring cup (never pack) and with a flat surface, like a butter knife, swipe the excess across the top. This also applies to the *shugá*. The best way to measure is to use a food scale.

BEST BANANA BREAD

You may know this Banana Bread from my TikTok video that went viral, reaching more than 25.1 million views and 4.3 million likes to date. It has been featured in "The Year on TikTok: Top 100", and as a finalist for "Top TikTok Food Trends of 2020." What makes this banana bread is the main ingredient, bananas! The particular ripeness is what makes this bread the best! You want many brown spots but they shouldn't be rotted. Two cups (450 g) of mashed bananas is ideal for a very moist bread, I've even used 3 cups (675 g) but I don't recommend it, because you may run into problems getting it to set. Grab an oven thermometer next time you're at the grocery store or kitchen store and fix it onto your oven rack permanently. Most of our ovens need to be calibrated and this is a way to ensure your oven reads exactly the temperature you need to bake the best banana bread!

Makes 1 loaf

1½ cups (188 g) all-purpose flour

1 tsp baking soda

½ tsp kosher salt

¾ cup (168 g) unsalted butter, softened

1 cup (220 g) packed light brown sugar

2 large eggs, room temperature

1½–2 cups (338–450 g) mashed ripe bananas (3–4 small bananas)

1 tsp pure vanilla extract

Chefie Tip:
After 50 minutes, if the top is browned and the center is still not set, loosely tent the top with foil and continue baking for another 10 to 15 minutes, until set.

Preheat the oven to 350°F (175°C) and spray a 9 x 5–inch (23 x 13–cm) loaf pan with baking spray and set aside.

Sift the flour and baking soda into a large bowl. Add the salt and whisk to combine. Set aside.

In a stand mixer fitted with the paddle attachment, cream the butter and brown *shugá* on medium speed until combined. Add one egg at a time and blend until combined. Add the bananas and vanilla and continue mixing on medium-high speed until combined, scraping down the sides as needed.

Pour the flour mixture onto the center of a piece of parchment or wax paper, in a straight line about 18 inches (46 cm) long lengthwise. Carefully pick up the paper and slowly funnel in the flour, a little bit at a time, on low speed. This way, the flour won't waft all over you and make a mess. Gradually increase the speed to medium, scraping down the sides and under the bottom of the bowl's dimple, as needed until blended. Don't overmix!

Pour the mixture into the prepared loaf pan and bake until the center is set, 50 to 60 minutes (see Chefie Tip). To check doneness, insert a long wooden skewer all the way to the bottom of the bread. If it comes out clean, the bread is ready. Remove the bread from the oven and let it cool in the pan, 1 to 2 hours. Don't rip into it right away, it'll fall apart!

MINT CHOCOLATE CHIP COOKIES

Peppermint extract gives these cookies an authentic Mint Chocolate Chip flavor, whereas mint extract tastes like toothpaste. Don't substitute! The green color screams mint and makes them fun for both St. Patrick's Day and Christmas.

Makes 40 cookies

¾ cup (168 g) unsalted butter, softened

1¼ cups (250 g) sugar

2 large eggs

1 tsp peppermint extract

2½ cups (313 g) all-purpose flour

1 tsp baking soda

½ tsp baking powder

½ tsp kosher salt

10–20 drops green food coloring

1 cup (215 g) chopped Andes Creme de Menthe thins or baking chips

1 cup (168 g) semi-sweet chocolate chips

Preheat the oven to 350°F (175°C). Line a baking sheet with parchment paper or a silicone mat.

In a stand mixer fitted with the paddle attachment, cream the butter and *shugá* on medium speed until combined, about 2 minutes. Add the eggs and peppermint extract and mix on medium-low speed until combined, 30 seconds. Increase the speed to medium and mix for 1 to 2 minutes until blended. Scrape down the sides as needed.

Whisk the flour, baking soda, baking powder and salt in a large bowl to combine. Pour the flour mixture onto the center of a piece of parchment or wax paper, in a straight line about 18 inches (46 cm) long lengthwise. Carefully pick up the paper and slowly funnel in the flour, a little bit at a time, on low speed. This way, the flour won't waft all over you and make a mess. Scrape down the sides and under the dimple as needed. Carefully add the food coloring, starting with 10 drops, and mix on low speed until blended. Add a few more drops at a time, if needed, until the color is mint green.

Stir in the Andes candies and chocolate chips until evenly combined.

Using a cookie scoop or heaping tablespoon measure, drop the cookie batter, spaced 2 to 3 inches (5 to 8 cm) apart so they don't melt together, onto the baking sheet. You will be able to fit eight to ten cookies per sheet. Bake for 10 to 12 minutes. Remove the cookies from the sheet and put them on a cooling rack to fully cool. Repeat with the remaining dough.

BAKLAVA *with* ORANGE SYRUP

My husband is half Greek Cypriot. In fact, we were married in Cyprus 21 years ago. When I met his extended family, I immediately fell in love with them and their culture. They're so loving and warm and family is always surrounded by a home-cooked meal, every day! Just the way it should be. When I created my take on baklava, I adjusted the height of the layers to make it more bite-size friendly and reduced the amount of *shugá* so it wasn't as sweet, but added a freshness, using orange juice and zest. My father-in-law took one bite and said, "This is the best baklava I've ever had!" Whoa! I was beaming with joy!

If using store-bought phyllo dough, use half of a (16-ounce (454-g)) package (20 sheets) and after you're feeling confident, try your hand at making the phyllo from scratch, don't be afraid!

Makes 12 servings

1 cup (120 g) chopped pecans

1 cup (117 g) chopped walnuts

2 tsp (3 g) ground cinnamon

¼ tsp kosher salt

1 cup (2 sticks (224 g)) unsalted butter, melted, kept warm

10 (9 x 14–inch (23 x 36–cm)) homemade phyllo pastry sheets (page 18)

Zest of 2 oranges

½ cup (120 ml) freshly squeezed orange juice

2 cinnamon sticks

1¼ cups (250 g) granulated sugar

Confectioners' sugar, to garnish

Preheat the oven to 375°F (190°C).

In a food processor fitted with the steel blade attachment, pulse the nuts, cinnamon and salt to finely grind. Do not purée at high speed or the nuts will turn into nut butter. Set aside.

Grab a 9 x 12 x 2–inch (23 x 30 x 5–cm) baking dish and using a pastry brush, lightly brush the baking dish with the melted butter over the bottom and up the sides to evenly coat—a little goes a long way.

Unroll the phyllo onto a work surface. Work with one phyllo sheet at a time, keeping the remaining sheets covered with a clean dish towel so they don't dry out and crack. Place the first phyllo sheet onto the bottom of the baking dish, then quickly re-cover the remaining phyllo with the kitchen towel.

Drizzle a little more butter over the phyllo in the baking dish, then carefully brush the phyllo sheet to evenly coat with a thin layer of butter. Repeat this procedure with three more phyllo sheets (six more if using store-bought phyllo), buttering between each layer. Scatter half of the nut mixture evenly on top of the phyllo.

(Continued)

BAKLAVA *with* ORANGE SYRUP (*continued*)

Repeat with three more buttered layers of phyllo (or seven more if using store-bought phyllo), buttering each layer as before, then scatter the remaining nut mixture evenly over the top and finish with the last three layers (six layers if using store-bought), buttering each sheet of phyllo. Drizzle the rest of the butter over the top sheet and brush the top phyllo sheet.

Using a sharp knife, score and cut through the phyllo, making 12 squares or 16 triangles. Bake until the top is golden brown, 23 to 25 minutes.

While the baklava is baking, make the orange syrup. Add the orange zest, juice, cinnamon sticks, granulated *shugá* and 1 cup (240 ml) of water to a 2-quart (1.9-L) saucepan and bring to a rapid bubble over medium-high heat, stirring until the *shugá* is melted. Cook the mixture until it has thickened and coats the back of a spoon, similar to the consistency of pure maple syrup, 12 to 18 minutes. You should have 1 cup (240 ml) of syrup, a little tip to know you've reduced it enough.

Remove the pan from the heat, discard the zest and cinnamon sticks and slightly cool to room temperature.

When you remove the baklava from the oven, cut the phyllo through the same cuts you made before baking to make sure each piece is fully cut through. Immediately pour the slightly cooled orange syrup over the hot baklava; the baklava will bubble but as it cools it will slowly absorb the syrup.

Let the baklava sit at room temperature to cool. Garnish with confectioners' *shugá* before serving, makes it pretty!

Chefie Tip:

HERE IS YOUR CHEAT SHEET FOR LAYERING THE PHYLLO:

Homemade Phyllo: 4 sheets phyllo, half of nut mixture, 3 sheets phyllo, remaining nut mixture, 3 sheets phyllo

Store-Bought Phyllo: 7 sheets phyllo, half of nut mixture, 7 sheets phyllo, remaining nut mixture, 6 sheets phyllo

PECAN PIE *with* CRÈME CHANTILLY

Ever since I was a little girl, my mom has made this pie every year for Thanksgiving. I would never eat it, I couldn't get past the brown color. As the years went on and I kept hearing my family make a fuss over it, I decided to taste it. One bite led to me eating the entire pie! 'Nuff said! I've been making it ever since.

Here's my version inspired by my mom's delicious pecan filling; I've added a homemade crust and crème Chantilly. It's French! This sweetened whipped cream flavored with vanilla is named after the town of Chantilly, near Paris, where it was created.

Makes 1 pie, 8 servings

FOR THE PIE CRUST

1½ cups (188 g) all-purpose flour + extra for dusting

½ tsp kosher salt

4 tbsp (56 g) cold unsalted butter, small dice

4 tbsp (45 g) cold vegetable shortening, cut into small dollops

FOR THE FILLING

3 large eggs

1 cup (240 ml) dark corn syrup

½ cup (100 g) sugar

½ cup (1 stick [112 g]) unsalted butter, melted, cooled

1 tsp pure vanilla extract

1¼ cups (150 g) pecan halves

In a food processor fitted with the blade attachment, pulse the flour and salt a few times to combine. Evenly scatter the butter and shortening pieces over the flour and pulse several times until the mixture has a sandy texture. Slowly pour 3 to 4 tablespoons (45 to 60 ml) of ice-cold water through the feed tube on high speed until the dough begins to form a ball; this will happen quickly. Immediately stop adding the water and stop the food processor as the ball whips around. Remove the dough ball and place on a floured surface to flatten the dough into a ½-inch (1.3-cm)-thick disk. Wrap the dough in plastic wrap and refrigerate until chilled, 1 hour to overnight.

When the dough is chilled, place it on a lightly floured surface and roll into an 11-inch (28-cm) circle. Carefully pick up the dough, place it in a 9-inch (23-cm) pie plate and roll the excess border of the crust under. Using two fingers, pinch a zigzag shape to form the crust edges. Chill the pie crust in the refrigerator while preparing the filling.

Preheat the oven to 375°F (190°C). In a stand mixer fitted with the paddle attachment, add the eggs and beat on low speed. Slowly pour in the dark corn syrup and continue beating, increasing the speed to medium, mixing until combined.

(Continued)

PECAN PIE *with* CRÈME CHANTILLY *(continued)*

FOR THE CRÈME CHANTILLY

1 cup (240 ml) cold heavy cream

3 tbsp (24 g) confectioners' sugar

1 tsp pure vanilla extract

Add the *shugá*, butter and vanilla and mix on medium-high speed, until well combined. DO NOT let the mixture get frothy—it'll make the pecans sink when baking. The pie looks prettier when the pecans rise to the top. Scatter the pecans over the bottom of the pie dough and pour the filling mixture over the pecans. Bake until the filling is set, with a slight wiggle in the center, 40 to 45 minutes. Place the pie on a cooling rack to cool completely.

While the pie is baking, clean the mixing bowl and run it under cold water to chill the bowl before drying. A chilled bowl will help to make a fluffy whipped cream. To make the crème Chantilly, in the chilled bowl of a stand mixer, mix the cold cream, confectioners' *shugá* and vanilla by hand, using the whisk attachment from the mixer. Then, fit the whisk onto the stand mixer and whisk on low speed until the cream begins to slightly thicken. Increase the speed to medium-high until medium (but not stiff) peaks form, 1 to 2 minutes. Scoop the cream into a bowl and cover. Keep refrigerated until ready to use; it's best to serve same day.

You can make the pie 1 day ahead and keep in a cool, dry place. When you're ready to serve, slice the pie into eight wedges and dollop with desired amount of crème Chantilly.

RED VELVET CUPCAKES

The white vinegar in this recipe does two things; it helps the baking soda react for a tender cupcake and also preserves the beautiful red color. Make sure to remove the cream cheese and butter to room temperature 2 hours before you want to make the frosting so you don't have little flecks of hard butter and cream cheese in the icing.

Makes 16 cupcakes

2½ cups (313 g) all-purpose flour

1½ tsp (7 g) baking soda

¾ tsp baking powder

1 tsp kosher salt

1½ cups (360 ml) buttermilk

1½ cups (300 g) granulated sugar

½ cup (120 ml) canola or vegetable oil

3 large eggs, room temperature

1 tsp pure vanilla extract

1 tsp white distilled vinegar

1 tbsp (15 ml) red food coloring

Cream Cheese Frosting (page 140)

Preheat the oven to 375°F (190°C). Line two (12-cup) muffin pans with 16 cupcake baking cups.

Sift the flour, baking soda and baking powder into a large bowl, add the salt and whisk to combine. Set aside.

Add the buttermilk, *shugá*, oil, eggs, vanilla extract, vinegar and red food coloring to the bowl of a stand mixer fitted with the whisk attachment. Begin mixing on low speed until the mixture comes together, then increase the speed to medium and mix until blended.

Pour the flour mixture onto the center of a piece of parchment or wax paper, in a straight line about 18 inches (46 cm) long lengthwise. Carefully pick up the paper and slowly funnel in the flour, a little bit at a time, on low speed. This way, the flour won't waft all over you and make a mess. Gradually increase the speed to medium, scraping down the sides and under the bottom of the bowl's dimple, as needed until blended. Don't overmix!

Divide the batter among the baking cups, filling three-quarters of the way. Let the batter rest, 10 minutes, to relax the gluten. Bake until the tops and center are set and a toothpick comes out clean, 15 to 17 minutes. (Now is a good time to make the frosting.)

Remove the cupcakes from the oven. When they're cool enough to handle, take them out of the muffin pans and place them on a cooling rack to cool. Place the frosting into a piping bag, fitted with a 1M star tip. Don't overfill the bag, you'll have better control when it's filled about two-thirds of the way. Frost the cupcakes.

GINGERBREAD MILKSHAKE

This recipe came to be because my son, Costas, loved getting these from a burger joint we often went to, and I thought, I can do that at home . . . but better. I use premium ice cream to re-create this with my own spin. This shake is great to enjoy during the fall season, while everyone is OD-ing on pumpkin, including me; it's another festive, feel-good treat.

Makes 1 (12-oz [355-ml]) milkshake

14 oz (1¾ cups (397 g))
premium vanilla ice cream
(I love Häagen-Dazs)

¼ cup (60 ml) whole milk, cold

½ tsp pure vanilla extract

¼ tsp ground cinnamon + extra
to garnish

2 ginger snap cookies or
spiced wafers

3 ice cubes

Crème Chantilly (page 159), to
garnish

Add the ice cream, milk, vanilla, cinnamon, cookies and ice cubes to a blender and blend until smooth, occasionally stopping the blender to stir the mixture, as needed, to get it moving. Resist the urge to add more milk! It'll be thick at first and may need some coaxing, but it'll begin to blend and make a thick, delicious shake.

Pour the shake into a tall glass and pipe crème Chantilly on top. Sprinkle with a dash of *cinny-mon*, because you're fancy! Serve immediately with a big (smoothie-size) straw.

Chefie Tip:
Pastry bags and 1M star tips can be found at craft stores or kitchen stores. It'll make you look profesh!

PECAN CANDY

These are quick and easy to make, but don't try to film a vid for your Insta story, because you'll screw them up. Ha. Yeah, that was me many times, trying to get that sexy, candy lava pouring from the pot. Once you remove the hot candied pecans from the pot, you need to move quickly to separate them or they'll be in one giant clump. The baking soda helps make the candy coating easy on your teeth but with a nice crackle crunch. Serve these candies on a cheese board because you're fancy or for snacking with cocktails. They taste like little pecan pie bites without the crust. Beware, they're addicting!

Makes 2 cups (200 g)

2 cups (200 g) pecan halves (no broken pieces)

4 tbsp (56 g) unsalted butter

⅔ cup (132 g) granulated sugar

½ cup (110 g) packed light brown sugar

1 tbsp (15 ml) light corn syrup

2 tbsp (30 ml) half and half

¾ tsp kosher salt

¼ tsp baking soda

Chefie Tip:
As soon as the candy begins to harden, stop pulling the pecans apart; if you continue trying to stretch it'll make the candy cloudy and we want it shiny and pretty. Once hardened, the pecans break apart easily.

Secure a long piece of parchment paper so it doesn't slide onto a surface that's not a marble or stone countertop surface. The cold surface will make it difficult to separate the candy pecans. Preferably, use a silicone baking mat.

Preheat the oven to 300°F (150°C). Arrange the pecans on a small rimmed baking sheet and warm through, about 5 minutes.

While the pecans are warming, melt the butter in a 2½-quart (2.4-L) saucepan over medium heat. Add the *shugás*, corn syrup, half and half and salt. Stir until dissolved, using a rubber spatula. Attach a candy thermometer inside the pot, making sure the bulb reaches the mixture but is not touching the bottom of the pot.

Bring the mixture to a bubble over medium heat. Cook until the candy thermometer reaches 280°F (140°C; the soft cracked stage), 4 to 5 minutes. Remove the pan from the heat and immediately stir in the baking soda, then stir in the warmed pecans until they are evenly coated. Work quickly! Immediately remove the pecans to the prepared piece of parchment paper or silicone mat. Using two forks, quickly separate the pecans, spreading them apart. As soon as the sauce begins tightening, stop!

Let the pecans set at room temperature to cool completely. Once cooled, break the pecan pieces apart. Serve immediately or store in an airtight container and refrigerate for up to 2 weeks.

CRAFTY COCKTAILS

When I was in my early twenties, I attended mixology school to learn how to make cocktails. I crafted fun drinks in nightclubs; created fancy martinis in a martini bar; and made perfectly frothy, boozy cappuccinos in an Italian restaurant for several years. It got me through college, plus I loved it! It's so much fun making cocktails, and there's nothing better than when they're made fresh. If you have an electric juicier, it makes it easier and quicker to juice fruit, but your food processor does the trick too. You'll just need to strain the juice in a cheesecloth to remove any pulp. Texture is important, but don't stress over it. It's easy! I'll show you.

We'll make not one but two margaritas because they're my favorite. I'll show you how to make the perfect Jalapeño Mezcal Margaritas (page 168) with just the right amount of chile flavor that enhances it without being overpowering and another Margie—I like to call them Margies—that is for the holiday season: My Merry Margaritas (page 179) are festive and reminiscent of Christmas.

I love a martini glass; there's something about the hand's feeling on the stem while sipping just enough from the slanted cold edge of the glass that makes me feel sexy. Here're two to make you feel sensual: my beloved Candy Apple Martinis (page 176) and Sexy Sidecars (page 171).

When entertaining, choose one signature cocktail, make a batch (or two, wink) ahead, keep covered in the refrigerator for hours and when your company arrives, pour, shake and serve! Don't play bartender, it's too stressful. It's your party, too!

JALAPEÑO MEZCAL MARGARITAS

I've found muddling the jalapeño slices makes this cocktail unenjoyable and way too spicy, whereas stirring in a few slices right before serving adds a beautiful flavoring of jalapeño with a mild zip midway through sipping. Don't forget the salt! A pinch heightens the *flavah!* Mezcal is a distilled alcohol made from agave; makes it smokey!

Makes 4 (6-oz [177-ml]) cocktails

8 oz (237 ml) blanco tequila

4 oz (118 ml) Cointreau

2 oz (59 ml) mezcal

⅔ cup (160 ml) freshly squeezed lime juice (from 4–6 limes; see Chefie Tips)

½ cup (120 ml) simple syrup (see Chefie Tips)

Kosher salt

4 tsp (1 g) chopped cilantro, divided

8–12 slices from 1 fresh jalapeño

In a medium pitcher, add the tequila, Cointreau, mezcal, lime juice and simple syrup and stir until well blended.

Fill four rocks glasses with ice. Fill a cocktail shaker with ice and add half of the margarita mixture and a pinch of salt. Shake vigorously for 30 seconds and strain among two prepared rocks glasses. Add a few more ice cubes to the cocktail shaker, if needed, and repeat with the remaining mixture. Don't forget the pinch of salt!

Divide the cilantro and jalapeño slices among the glasses and give each a stir.

Chefie Tips:

To make simple syrup, melt 1 cup (200 g) *shugá* with 1 cup (240 ml) water in a 2-quart (1.9-L) saucepan. Bring to a bubble over high heat and stir until syrupy, 4 to 6 minutes. Chill until ready to use.

Roll the lime before squeezing, it loosens the juice.

SEXY SIDECARS

I love a good cocktail and this one has been a favorite of mine for a couple years now. The key to a good concoction is balance. You shouldn't taste the harsh alcohol flavor punching you in the face, but it shouldn't be weak either and fresh lemon juice is mandatory! Cointreau is an orange-flavored liqueur. It's French!

Makes 4 (about 8-oz [237-ml]) cocktails

1 cup (240 ml) freshly squeezed lemon juice (from 5–7 large lemons); reserve a squeezed lemon half to moisten the glass rim

¼ cup (60 ml) agave nectar

Sugar in the raw or turbinado sugar

12 oz (355 ml) cognac

8 oz (237 ml) Cointreau

Whisk the lemon juice and agave in a medium pitcher until blended.

Cut the halved squeezed lemon into wedges and moisten the rim of four martini glasses. Pour the *shugá* onto a rimmed plate, then dip the moistened rim of the martini glasses into the *shugá*, to evenly coat all the way around, shaking off the excess. Pour the cognac and Cointreau into the pitcher with the agave-lemon juice and stir well to combine.

Fill a cocktail shaker with ice and add half of the sidecar mixture. Shake vigorously for 30 seconds until it's very cold. We want ice crystals! Pour among two prepared martini glasses. Refill the cocktail shaker with ice, as needed, and repeat with the remaining mixture.

RASPBERRY MOJITOS

Mojitos are a light, slightly sweet and refreshing drink from Cuba. Pronounced koo-ba, not cue-ba! I added fresh raspberries, because you can, and it makes it pretty. These are so tasty. *Salud!*

Makes 4 (7-oz [207-ml]) cocktails

6 oz (170 g) raspberries, divided

½ cup (100 g) granulated sugar

20 fresh mint leaves, divided + extra to garnish

8 oz (237 ml) premium white rum, divided

½ cup (120 ml) freshly squeezed lime juice (from about 2 limes), divided

Chilled club soda

1 lime, sliced

Set aside twelve raspberries (they're our garnish). To make the raspberry syrup, place the remaining raspberries, *shugá* and ½ cup (120 ml) water into a 2-quart (1.9-L) saucepan and bring to a rolling bubble over high heat. Mash the berries, using a potato masher or the back of a fork, and stir until the *shugá* is dissolved. Cook until syrupy, 3 to 4 minutes. Remove the pan from the stove and strain the mixture through a fine-mesh strainer over a heat-safe bowl, discarding the raspberry seeds. Let the mixture cool. You can make this up to 2 days ahead, cover and refrigerate.

Pierce three raspberries onto each cocktail pick, then repeat three more times, making four picks total. Fill four highball glasses with ice. Muddle ten mint leaves into a cocktail shaker to bruise and break up the leaves. Fill the shaker halfway with ice. Add 4 ounces (113 ml) of the rum, ¼ cup (60 ml) lime juice and half of the raspberry syrup. Shake vigorously for 30 seconds.

Strain among two prepared glasses and repeat the process with ten more mint leaves and the remaining rum, lime juice and raspberry syrup. Top off each glass with a few splashes of club soda. Garnish each glass with a slice of lime, sprig of mint and a raspberry pick—because you're fancy!

ORANGE-BERRY SANGRIA

This is my Thanksgiving sangria! Every year while I'm cranking out a huge holiday meal, this signature cocktail has been taken care of the day prior. Which is mandatory, for best *flavah!* Set out wine glasses, a bucket of ice and the pitcher of sangria and let everyone help themselves. Make sure you snag a glass first; it goes quick and everyone loves it, so you may wanna double or triple it!

I like Stirrings Apple Liqueur (it's green). It can be found at most liquor stores or online, but if you're having trouble finding it, you can substitute with sour apple pucker.

Makes 5 servings

1 small Granny Smith apple, cored, quartered and thinly sliced

1 small orange, quartered and thinly sliced

3 oz (85 g) fresh blackberries

3 oz (85 g) fresh raspberries

⅓ cup (80 ml) green apple liqueur

⅓ cup (80 ml) Cointreau

⅓ cup (80 ml) blackberry brandy

⅓ cup (80 ml) Chambord

1 (26-oz (770-ml)) bottle Grenache or Tempranillo

Place the apple and orange slices, blackberries and raspberries in the bottom of a large glass serving pitcher.

Pour the apple liqueur, Cointreau, blackberry brandy, Chambord and Grenache over the fruit and stir well. Cover and refrigerate to marinate 6 hours to overnight. Want the best *flavah?* Refrigerate overnight!

Fill five wine glasses halfway with ice and add a few pieces of the drunken fruit to the glasses. Pour sangria among the glasses.

CANDY APPLE MARTINIS

These are fantastic during the fall season—it's the adult version of a candy apple. Make a batch of this ahead of time; it'll take the stress off when entertaining! Keep the mixture in a medium pitcher and place it in the refrigerator. Prep your glasses with the *shugá* rim up to 15 minutes ahead. You don't want to do this too far ahead or it'll harden to the point where the *shugá* won't come off with each sip. We don't want that! Then shake and serve. Shake it baby! We want ice crystals! I like Stirrings Apple Liqueur (it's green). It can be found at most liquor stores or online, but if you're having trouble finding it, you can substitute with sour apple pucker.

Makes 4 (6-oz [177-ml]) cocktails

6 Granny Smith apples, divided

2 tbsp (30 ml) freshly squeezed lemon juice

½ lemon, cut into wedges

Red sanding sugar

6 oz (177 ml) premium vodka

4 oz (118 ml) green apple liqueur

2 oz (59 ml) grenadine

Chefie Tip:
For the garnish, you can slice the remaining apple ahead and squeeze *limón* juice over the slices. Tightly wrap plastic wrap directly on top of the slices, to suffocate them, so they don't turn brown.

Peel, core and chop five of the apples and place them in a food processor fitted with the steel blade attachment. Pour the lemon juice over the apples and purée until the apples are super fine and liquified. Pour the apple juice purée into a large bowl fully lined with a large piece of cheesecloth and fold the cheesecloth up and over the puréed apple mixture. Twist and wring, making a purse, squeezing out all the apple juice into the bowl. You'll have plenty of leftover juice to make more martinis, if you like (wink, I got you)!

Alternatively, you can purée the apples in a fruit/vegetable juicer, skim and discard the foam, then strain the juice through a fine-mesh strainer. Don't forget to add the lemon juice. You can prepare this up to 6 hours ahead, cover and refrigerate. If it starts to turn brown, donta you worry!

Moisten the rim of four martini glasses with the lemon wedges. Pour some of the *shugá* onto a rimmed plate, then dip the moistened rim of the martini glasses into the *shugá* to coat all the way around, shaking off the excess. Pour the vodka, apple liqueur, grenadine and 1 cup (240 ml) of the fresh apple juice into a large pitcher and stir well.

Fill a cocktail shaker with ice and add half of the candy apple martini mixture. Shake vigorously for 30 seconds, we want ice crystals! Pour among two prepared martini glasses. Refill the cocktail shaker with ice and repeat with the remaining mixture. Thinly slice the remaining apple and garnish each martini with one slice—because you're fancy!

MERRY MARGARITAS

Every year I receive a huge box of cranberries straight from the bog, so I purposely find reasons to use them for anything and everything I can conjure up. A few years back, during the holiday season I created this one. The rosemary is not just a holiday garnish, it plays a great role lending a hint of *flavah* to the cocktail. It intrigues your senses with each sip as you lift the glass to your lips with the piney, herb aroma pleasantly wafting holiday cheer.

After straining the cranberries to make the homemade cranberry syrup, I sweeten them with *shugá* and a dash of ground *cinny-mon* to make cranberry jam. Cover and refrigerate until well chilled. Serve the cranberry jam with sharp cheddar cheese and crackers. This recipe is two-in-one for your holiday entertaining made easy.

Makes 4 (7-oz [207-ml]) cocktails

¾ cup (150 g) sugar, divided
2 cups (200 g) fresh whole cranberries
¼ tsp ground cinnamon

Add 1½ cups (360 ml) cold water and ½ cup (100 g) *shugá* to a 2-quart (1.9-L) saucepan and bring to a bubble over high heat. Stir the *shugá* until dissolved. Reduce the heat to medium and add the cranberries except for 12 of them, we need those to garnish. Set them aside.

Cook the cranberry mixture until syrupy and the cranberries break, 5 minutes, stirring periodically. Transfer the cranberry syrup to a fine-mesh strainer over a heat-safe bowl or pitcher. Strain, pushing the mixture's liquid through the mesh strainer using a spoon, mashing the cranberries. Remove the mashed cranberries to a small bowl and stir 3 tablespoons (45 g) *shugá* and the cinnamon into the jam until the *shugá* is melted. Cover and refrigerate the jam until well chilled. Add the 12 cranberries to the cranberry simple syrup, cover and refrigerate until the syrup is well chilled. It's best to soak the cranberries overnight for tasty garnishes. The cranberry syrup will yield about 1½ cups (360 ml).

(Continued)

MERRY MARGARITAS *(continued)*

4 rosemary sprigs (6–7 inches (15–18 cm) long)

1 cup (240 ml) good-quality blanco tequila

⅔ cup (160 ml) Cointreau

⅓ cup (80 ml) freshly squeezed lime juice (from 2–3 limes)

Meanwhile, to prepare the garnishes, when the twelve cranberries are chilled and soaked, pierce three cranberries onto a decorative skewer, then repeat three more times, making four skewers. The skewers should be long enough to rest on top of the rim of the glasses. Sprinkle the remaining 1 tablespoon (15 g) *shugá* onto a plate and roll the sticky cranberries in the *shugá*, coating all the way around. Set the prepared skewers on a wax- or parchment paper–lined plate. Wet each rosemary sprig with cold water, shaking off the excess. Lightly roll each sprig in the *shugá* and place on the plate with the cranberry skewers. Keep refrigerated until ready to serve.

Into a medium pitcher, pour the tequila, Cointreau, lime juice and 1½ cups (360 ml) of cranberry simple syrup and stir well. You can make this up to several hours ahead; keep covered in the refrigerator.

Fill four stemmed margarita or rocks glasses with ice. Stir the cranberry margarita mixture, then pour among the glasses and arrange each prepared rosemary sprig, dipped halfway inside the glasses, to infuse the rosemary flavor. Place the cranberry skewers across the rim of the glasses.

Serve the cranberry jam in a small bowl on a cheese board with a good sharp cheddar cheese and crackers, for spreading.

Acknowledgments

It's been a dream of mine since I was a young girl to write cookbooks and share my passion for cooking homemade food to make people feel happy; because of you this book was possible. I want to thank each and every one of my followers on TikTok, Instagram, Facebook, YouTube, Twitter and my website. I love you guys and appreciate you more than you'll ever know! Continue sending me food photos and videos, I'm so proud of you! Keep Cooking from Scratch . . . Because You Can!

My father, who at the age of two contracted polio, which left him permanently handicapped, went on to build our family home with no experience and restore antique cars from nothing to perfection. His talent, creativity, strong will and determination I've always looked up to and respected. I love you Daddy, always and forever! I'll miss you deeply, today is bittersweet for me, but I know that you're smiling as you enter heaven so proud of your baby girl, that you begged Mom to have just one more child because you wanted me, a girl. Thank you for the gift of life, talent and creativity to create with my heart and hands. To my mother, I'm so proud to share our family recipes that you always warmed our hearts with.

I've been developing and testing recipes for as long as I've been cooking, which is from birth, ha ha. Just kidding, it has been a long time though. My son, Costas, and daughter, Isabella, are refined taste testers with very keen palates, and did I mention zero filter? We're Greek and Italian, so they let it rip! I'm thankful for your honesty, good and bad—we're a team! I love you both!

To my girlfriend and chefie sidekick, Jeannette, I'm incredibly thankful for you in more ways than one, and there's no way I could have ever prepped, cooked and styled sixty recipes in five days without you! You are everything! I love you . . . plus, you've got great knife skills, too!

Ken Goodman, you're a rockstar! How did I get so lucky to get to work with you? I'm beyond grateful for your commitment, passion and creativity. My photos rock! We made a great team!

To my girlfriend Barbie, thank you for pulling me up every time I needed you; your recipe testing came at a time I needed you most! To Jaclyn and her team at True Aussie Beef & Lamb for selflessly devoting their time to recipe test, I appreciate you all!

(Continued)

Acknowledgments (Continued)

My mother-in-law, mommy, the perfect angel. You always believed in me and you'd be over the moon right now, telling all our Italian and Greek cousins. I can only imagine how you're driving them crazy in heaven. They're probably sick of hearing my name, lol. To my father-in-law, babá, which means father. It's Greek! Thank you for treating me like your very own daughter. I make great Greek food because of you!

When I received the email from my editor, wait: Did I just say my editor? I still can't believe it! I cried. Tears streaming down my face. At this point in my career, I never thought it was actually going to happen, so NEVER GIVE UP ON YOUR DREAMS, *EVAH!* Thank you, Marissa Giambelluca, for believing in me!

Thank you to the team at Page Street Publishing, for taking the time to work one on one with me to publish a beautifully created book.

To my husband, Andreas, who when our children were little took over caring for them so I could travel back and forth to New York City to attend culinary school, to pursue my passion that burned in my heart, as you juggled your hectic on-call schedule caring for your patients. Thank you for your love and support of twenty-one years, believing in me and lifting me as I spread my wings. You're my soul mate! Plus, you love food, we're a perfect match!

About the Author

Shereen Pavlides is a recipe developer and international social media personality and chef influencer reaching millions worldwide, inspiring her followers to cook from scratch . . . because they can! She is an honors graduate of the Institute of Culinary Education in New York City and has worked as a food stylist and on-air product host for QVC; as a food writer and host of Cook This! with Shereen, a digital cooking show for GateHouse Media; and as a recipe developer and culinary consultant for corporate test kitchens.

She's appeared on ABC's *Good Morning America* and *Tamron Hall Show*; on CBS's *The Doctors*; in *People*, *Teen Vogue*, Tasty and BuzzFeed, in addition to being featured in "The Year on TikTok: Top 100," as a finalist for "Top TikTok Food Trends of 2020." Follow her on Instagram, TikTok, Facebook and YouTube @CookingwithShereen or on Twitter @ShereenPavlides.

Index